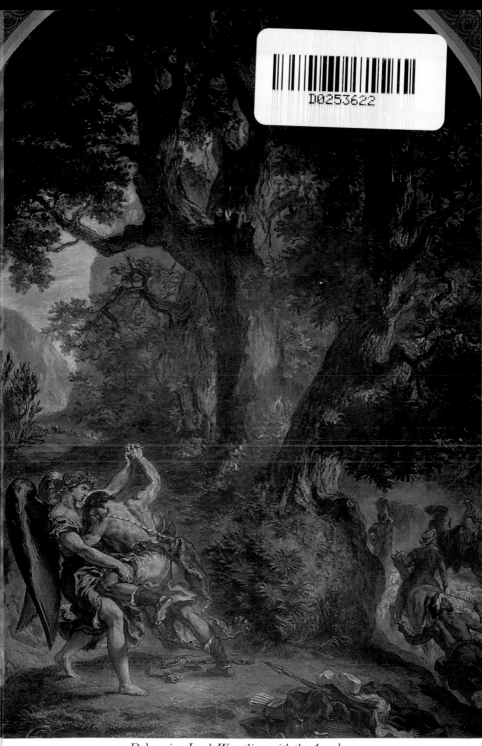

Delacroix: *Jacob Wrestling with the Angel*

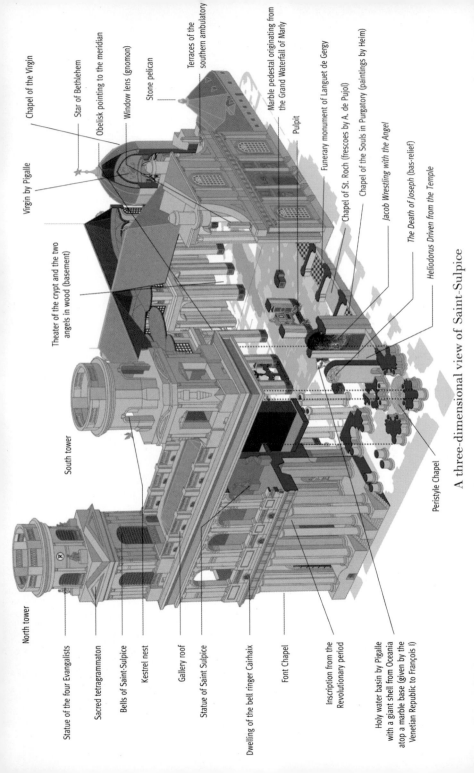

A three-dimensional view of Saint-Sulpice

RÉALISATION J.S.I.

Chapel of the Virgin

Star of Bethlehem

Obelisk pointing to the meridian

Window lens (gnomon)

Stone pelican

Terraces of the southern ambulatory

Marble pedestal originating from the Grand Waterfall of Marly

Funerary monument of Languet de Gergy

Pulpit

Chapel of St. Roch (frescoes by A. de Pujol)

Chapel of the Souls in Purgatory (paintings by Heim)

Jacob Wrestling with the Angel

The Death of Joseph (bas-relief)

Heliodorus Driven from the Temple

Virgin by Pigalle

Theater of the crypt and the two angels in wood (basement)

South tower

North tower

Statue of the four Evangalists

Sacred tetragrammaton

Bells of Saint-Sulpice

Kestrel nest

Gallery roof

Statue of Saint Sulpice

Dwelling of the bell ringer Cairhaix

Font Chapel

Inscription from the Revolutionary period

Holy water basin by Pigalle with a giant shell from Oceania atop a marble base (given by the Venetian Republic to François I)

Peristyle Chapel

ABOUT THE AUTHOR

JEAN-PAUL KAUFFMANN was a foreign correspondent when he was imprisoned in Beirut (May 1985 to May 1988). He is the author of *The Arch of Kerguelen* and *The Black Room at Longwood*, which was a finalist for the National Book Critics Circle Award. *The Angel of the Left Bank* was a bestseller in France, where it was a finalist for the prestigious Prix Goncourt. Kauffmann lives in Paris.

ABOUT THE TRANSLATOR

PATRICIA CLANCY is a prize-winning translator and lives in Melbourne, Australia.

The Angel of the Left Bank

Jean-Paul Kauffmann

The Angel of
the Left Bank

The Secrets of Delacroix's Parisian Masterpiece

Translated from the French by
Patricia Clancy

Random House Trade Paperbacks
New York

2004 Random House Trade Paperback Edition

This work was originally published in French by Editions de la Table Ronde,
Paris, in 2001. This English translation was originally published under the title
The Struggle With the Angel by Four Walls Eight Windows, New York, in 2002.
This edition published by arrangement with Four Walls Eight Windows.

Library of Congress Cataloging-in-Publication Data

Kauffmann, Jean-Paul.
[Lutte avec l'ange. English]
The angel of the Left Bank: the secrets of Delacroix's Parisian masterpiece /
Jean-Paul Kauffmann.
p.   cm.
Previously published as: The struggle with the angel. New York: Four Walls Eight
Windows c 2002
Includes bibliographical references and index.
ISBN 0-8129-7086-1
1. Delacroix, Eugéne, 1798–1863. Jacob wrestling with the angel. 2. Delacroix,
Eugéne, 1798–1863—Criticism and interpretation. 3. Mural painting and decora-
tion, French—France—Paris. 4. Saint-Sulpice (Church: Paris, France) I. Title.

ND553.D33A648 2004
759.4—dc22   2003058521

Random House website address: www.atrandom.com
Printed in the United States of America

9   8   7   6   5   4   3   2   1

First Trade Paperback Edition

For Grégoire and Alexandre

Jacob is travelling with the flocks and other gifts he is taking to his brother Esau in the hope of appeasing his anger. A stranger appears, blocking his path, and engages him in a fierce struggle which ends only when Jacob is struck on the nerve of his thigh by his adversary, rendering him powerless. The holy books see this struggle as a symbol of the trials God sometimes sends His chosen ones.

EUGÈNE DELACROIX[1]

Prologue

The leather-padded door bangs shut with a series of heavy thuds like the three knocks at the beginning of a play in the theater. The inside of the church is the same grey as old newspaper. Immediately on the right, the Chapel of the Holy Angels. The leaded window is plain glass. The only things that glow are the murals painted by Delacroix. *Jacob Wrestling with the Angel*, lit by natural daylight, is brighter than *Heliodorus Driven from the Temple*, which is often in shadow.

In this chapel, Delacroix has depicted one of the most puzzling passages in Genesis. Who is this adversary Jacob is fighting so vigorously? Is he an angel? Not only does the stranger refuse to defend himself, but he also faces the son of Isaac with disarming calm. He looks and acts like the victor. Yet at dawn, contrary to all expectation, Jacob has the upper hand. He prevails, but he is wounded for life. The grass on Jabbok and the foliage on the three tall trees are heavy with the dew of one of the first mornings of the world. The painting of Heliodorus opposite, drawn from the Book of the Maccabees, describes a scene of someone receiving a beating. Under the painting is a door that is nearly always closed.

Only daylight, preferably in the morning, can really bring out Delacroix's decorations of the chapel. The dirty grey of the church interior gives way to the diffused light of an aquarium:

the pallid green twilight of the seabed. In winter, from midday onward, it's better to forget this part of Saint-Sulpice. But on fine days—and I must admit to a liking for September—the church seems to sparkle. The smallest banks of cloud drifting across the sky, like the rising intensity of the sun, are reflected in the window. This liquid light shimmers like the ocean.

The Chapel of the Holy Angels is a mise-en-scène, as is the church that houses it. Parisians are not very keen on this theatrical house of God. One architect after another took a malicious pleasure in ignoring the work of his predecessor—and there were at least eight of them! They nevertheless failed to sabotage one of the most harmonious scenographies in the capital. Servandoni, set designer at the opera, king of scene shifters, genius at special effects, played a decisive role in all of this. Did he really botch the monumental facade? It is true that the cyclopean pillars overwhelm everything else. But this mistake has its good side: it discourages those who do not want to look any further than the proscenium.

In the nineteenth century, the sellers of devotional objects who had set up shop in the area invented the "Sulpician style," typified by plaster saints. In so doing, they created a regrettable confusion in people's minds. Many think that this form of effusive religiosity and bad taste also applies to the church itself. Nothing could be further from "Sulpician style" than the classical architecture of Saint-Sulpice.

The morning sun lighting up the square gives me a positive feeling of happiness. A heart is beating, even if it cannot be heard. There is an energy in that curiously layered architecture, a rhythm that gives a joyful character and a definite look of contentment to its rather heavy beauty and its obvious faults. It is an almost perfect church. Everything is contained in that "almost":

its appeal lies in its nonfulfilment, its incompleteness, symbolized by the two unfinished towers.

The church and the painting seem to me like two accomplices. They are in league with each other. What could they be hiding? I burst into the chapel like a detective turning up unexpectedly in search of a clue. All these patrols and investigations have yielded nothing so far, but I have not given up hope.

Two still sources of light glow in the church: the tabernacle lamp in the Chapel of the Virgin and the Delacroix panel in the Holy Angels. This light has flowed, unobstructed, for more than a century.

Acknowledgments

I should like to express my gratitude to the parish priest of Saint-Sulpice, Paul Roumanet. Many thanks also to Michel Portal. His knowledge of the church, his courtesy and generosity made my task very much easier.

I should also like to thank Jean-Paul Amat, Roselyne André, Michel Béal, Louis Bergès, Guy Bolsee, Chantal Bouchon, Robert Bougrain-Dubourg, Bernadette de Boysson, Georges Brunel, Imelda Brunerie, Michel Cantal-Dupart, Patrice Chagnard, Joseph Corbineau, Robert Couffignal, Christophe Cousin, Claudine and Paul Derome, Tancrède and Lô Dumont, Malika Fléau, Annick Fort, Bruno Foucart, Olivier Frébourg, Françoise Gaillard, Claude Hébert, Lydie Huyghe, Daniel Imbert, Sophie Join-Lambert, Béa Jomelli, Régis Labourdette, Nicole Lignac, Annie Lorenzo, Luc Monnet, Madeleine Neige, Irénée Noye, François Oubriot, Jean Pierrard, père Ploix, Noël Poncelin, Francis Ribemont, Gérard Rondeau, Georges Rose, Daniel Roth, Jean Schalit, Alain Ségal, Arlette Sérullaz, Charlotte Simon, Juliette Soulabaille, Denis Tillinac, and Isabelle Vazelle.

Finally, to Joëlle, who accompanied me in this long struggle, my most heartfelt thanks.

Table of Contents

And he rose up that night, and took his two wives, and his two women servants, and his eleven sons, and passed over the ford Jabbok. And he took them, and sent them over the brook, and sent over that he had. And Jacob was left alone; and there wrestled a man with him until the breaking of the day. And when he saw that he prevailed not against him, he touched the hollow of his thigh; and the hollow of Jacob's thigh was out of joint, as he wrestled with him. And he said, Let me go, for the day breaketh. And he said, I will not let thee go, except thou bless me. And he said unto him, What is thy name? And he said, Jacob. And he said, Thy name shall be called no more Jacob, but Israel: for as a prince hast thou power with God and with men, and hast prevailed. And Jacob asked him, and said, Tell me, I pray thee, thy name. And he said, Wherefore is it that thou dost ask after my name? And he blessed him there. And Jacob called the name of the place Penuel: for I have seen God face to face, and my life is preserved. And as he passed over Penuel the sun rose upon him, and he halted upon his thigh. Therefore the children of Israel eat not the sinew which shrank, which is upon the hollow of the thigh, unto this day: because he touched the hollow of Jacob's thigh in the sinew that shrank.[2]

The Angel of the Left Bank

CHAPTER 1

The Servandoni Towers

"In the world's fading light /
The stairs of Delphi meet the void."

I am laboring up the spiral staircase in the north tower of Saint-Sulpice. There are squares of paper stuck to the walls. Pausing to read the maxims scrawled on them gives my respiration a certain rhythm and allows me to catch my breath.

Who put up those two lines of poetry? The sacristan leading the way climbs the stairs effortlessly with a spring in his step. He is an impassive, laconic man, but his ability to observe and anticipate makes me think of a hunter. He has a very reliable instinct for anything to do with his church. He can find his way with no difficulty at all through the complicated network of galleries, secret passages, cellars, nooks, and crannies that make up the invisible face of the church. He is the keeper of the keys. He, better than anyone else, can gauge the progress of the insidious disease afflicting Saint-Sulpice: damp. It attacks the stone, crumbles the mortar, eats at the metal framework, and makes holes in the roofing.

"Saint-Sulpice is in danger of collapsing, and this is an understatement," warned the mayor of the sixth *arrondissement* in a letter to the prefect of Paris in 1900.

As the construction of the building has never been completed, it has been encumbered with temporary structures for three centuries. At the beginning of the Revolution, poles and scaffolding had still not been removed from the south tower, even though work had ceased a long time ago. The newspaper *Le Matin* announced triumphantly on 22 January 1912 that "The most famous scaffolding and also the oldest, as its origin is lost in the mists of time—that of Saint-Sulpice—has finally been taken down."

French ingenuity and love of tinkering struck again. The art of improvisation, that sin of national pride, wrought havoc here until the 1970s. It was thought that the problem with the building could be alleviated by repairing it with reinforced concrete. In the end, oxidation made the reinforcement swell until it split the stone.

The slow destruction of the building is heartbreaking for the sacristan. He coldly analyzes the causes and stages of the disease, speaking in short, sharp sentences that only make his personal distress and feelings of anger all the more apparent. Saint-Sulpice, the poor old ship, can no longer be careened for repairs. It is disappearing before our eyes; it has taken off beyond our reach. It is going to die and does not want to be in the way. The two thick masts of the uneven towers show the presence of the massive square vessel on the town horizon. The sails of the sloping roofs and the jib of the domes give the ship an elegant momentum, but there is no denying it: the hull is rotten.

"Rotten! You're exaggerating. In bad repair, most certainly," my companion exclaims.

"You know this church of yours is in a bad way. Why try to cover things up?"

I like to provoke him to test the limits of his composure. He pauses on the staircase and watches me panting a few steps below.

"Save your breath. The north tower is 240 feet high."

I think of Huysmans and Durtal, the main character in *Là-Bas*.[1]

"Have you read *Là-Bas*?"

"No."

"You should. It's a satanic novel, and Saint-Sulpice comes into it. The hero does the same thing as we are doing now."

"And what is that?" he says politely.

His expressionless voice gives no indication of curiosity. With his heavy build and open austere face, he is such an integral part of his church that one would think he was hewn from the very stone of Saint-Sulpice before it began to decline: a pure, tough limestone from the Creil region.

"Like us he climbs up the north tower where the bell ringer lives. Don't you think it strange that he could have imagined a detail like that?"

"Not so very strange! There *is* a room in the north tower. I'll show it to you."

Occasional openings in the wall let in patches of light to pierce the gloom and the noise of the town to ring in our ears. Then the hubbub reduces to a dull throb. The plaintive honking of car horns stands out above the general hum of the traffic. In the heart of Paris this distant noise is disturbing. As I climb higher, it slowly fades away. It emphasizes the fact that there is something missing, rather like the sounds heard by a prisoner that signify a life to which he no longer belongs.

We have reached the level of the second series of columns on top of the church facade. A drift of warm air smelling of dust and greasy wool—the heavy stale smell that lingers in the attic in summer—sometimes creeps into the staircase. Although I hold on to the continuous channel hollowed into the stone, which serves as a handrail, in the semidarkness my foot still hits against the rise of the next step. I stumble over dead birds, but these bodies of pigeons dried out by the weather are by no means repellent. They are so light that the tip of my shoe sends them into the air as if they were freeze-dried. The wind gusts in through the openings and whistles softly in my ears.

"How dreadful is this place!" Jacob declares when he wakes from his dream. He has seen a flight of stairs, and the top of it reaches to heaven.

As I climb I cannot help thinking about Jacob's dream, a story as enigmatic as the crossing at Jabbok, the ford where the fight with the angel takes place. The prophet Hosea makes a strange comparison of the two incidents: "He took his brother by the heel in the womb, and by his strength he had power with God: yea, he had power over the angel, and prevailed: he wept, and made supplication unto him: he found him in Beth-el."[2] It is at Bethel that Jacob has the dream about the ladder, a word that can be translated both as a ramp and a ziggurat.

Jacob is a marvelous symbol of what the French call *l'esprit de l'escalier*: thinking of what one should have said or done as one leaves and goes downstairs, when it is too late. For him events are nearly always delayed, when the right time has seemingly passed. His mother Rebecca, the barren wife, becomes a mother late in life. After she gives birth to Esau, the intruding twin suddenly appears: Jacob, the baby no one expected. He has lagged behind already, but he is also tenacious and very, very crafty. He has quietly taken a grip on Esau's heel. He clings on and will not be easily dislodged. His entry into the world bears all the signs of the usurper.

The sacristan's bunch of keys jingles with a happy silvery tinkle like a carillon. He opens a door, letting in a blast of air, then it bangs shut. For one moment I feel as if the wind-swept terrace is leading to a sheer drop. Paris suddenly appears below under our feet, silent, white, and strangely inert, spread out like a faded tapestry. A stony desert from which a rumbling sound rises up in waves. A monstrous, desolate vision of beautiful Sodom, spared by the angel but emptied of its inhabitants. There is something disturbing about it: a sense of suspended animation, the certainty that the whole scene will soon be no more, the premonition that everything has been played out. One can already foresee the final catastrophe. The grey concrete, the worn paving stones, this poor shaky, chalky mass will one day be buried in sand and silence. There will be only a few little peaks in a sierra of ruins. How long will the ziggurat of Saint-Sulpice hold out? A dry wind lifts ocher dust into the air. The Saint-Sulpice fountain gleams like a marble mausoleum surrounded by the dark clump of chestnut trees.

The sacristan looks at his watch. Suddenly there is such a loud explosion that I immediately think of a supersonic boom. The powerful shock wave seems to spread in slow motion, and the echo cannot settle in the air. This deep reverberation of sound rolls towards me. I'm stunned as it hits me full in the face, although the effect is more dizziness than a blow.

"That's Henriette," the sacristan says.

"Henriette?"

"Yes. A sharp!"

"I'm sorry. I don't understand what you mean."

"You'll also hear Thérèse and Caroline, A and B flat."

The second, deeper boom sends out a heavy sound in such a low register that I have to block my ears. Now I know why we had to move away from the tower. The bells of Saint-Sulpice are well-known for the redoubtable firepower of their sound. For this burst of energy with a huge incandescence that burns and devastates everything in its path is fire indeed. Its burning breath whips across my face. Once again the vibration makes me feel dizzy. I'm not afraid that I might fall over the edge; on the contrary, I feel a kind of paralysis overwhelming me, as if the ebb and flow that has ceased in the petrified world below is now spreading through me.

The most impressive thing is not Paris lying so still beneath our feet, but the last tier of the north tower with its statues of the four Evangelists. The clouds flying past skim the top and unravel into fleecy trails. Mark looks the most restless. The wear and tear of time and pollution have flattened his nose and ravaged his features. He has a violent face. He looks as if he might take off at any moment, straddle the flocks of clouds that look like woolly sheep, and ride them over to the other tower.

My companion, however, is looking elsewhere. He is examining the stones, investigating the progress of the disease.

"It's everywhere...Decades of seepage!" he says wearily.

"What can be done to save such a colossal edifice? The works that are carried out from time to time seem like patch-up jobs. It's just a pretence at helping this church!"

I know I'm exaggerating. The slate roof on the nave has been entirely replaced and the chapels on the south side of the ambulatory have been saved from damp. But no sooner has this curative surgery been applied to one limb than another part catches the disease. It is an impossible task to maintain the church and keep it in good condition. An operation is carried out only at the point of death. The keeper of the keys knows the hypocrisy of this intensive medication to keep the patient alive. He sees nonetheless that the tired old body is still holding out, and above all, he does not like to hear anyone speak ill of it.

"What do you know about it? Besides, it's not my department. You should ask the architects in the Historic Monuments Commission. Anyway, I thought you were interested in Delacroix's painting?"

"That's true...But there is a connection between them all. The painting can't be separated from the church. Saint-Sulpice, the Chapel of the Holy Angels, *Jacob Wrestling with the Angel*, they're all interrelated. Did you know that Delacroix painted the two towers when he was young and living in an attic in the rue Jacob? He was twenty-six."

He looks doubtful, and rightly so. But I won't give him my spiel about the theatrical side of Saint-Sulpice, or Servandoni, the opera set designer who planned the facade. His church, a mise-en-scène! I'm sure that would shock him. This sanctuary is the house of God; he is the official in charge of it. He certainly does not see himself in the role of a stagehand.

There is something elusive about Servandoni the painter, architect, set designer, man of the theater, adventurer. He invented the first diorama and devised the first sound and light show. Diderot considered the man "a great stage mechanic, a great architect, a good painter, and a sublime set artist." Nearly all his paintings have disappeared. Only a few of his canvases have been identified: a universe in ruins, tombs, burial pyramids in the style of Piranese. A world of archeology and dreams.

In the library of the École des Beaux-Arts in Paris there is a painting by Servandoni of Saint-Sulpice in ruins. The great door is broken and the famous fluted columns have been knocked down. It shows a very pronounced taste for theatrical effect.

The two strange towers are also represented, especially the unfinished south tower. It is riddled with holes and the sculptures are missing. One can make out the stone panels meant to house them.

*　　　*　　　*

"The New Temple of Solomon" was the name given to the building in the eighteenth century. "The Cloud of light which filled the Temple of Solomon on the day of its dedication as a sign that the Lord was taking possession of it, indicates here once again what happened but could not be seen at the consecration of that church."[3] What a strange comparison with the Jerusalem Temple, and no less strange the "invisible" sign that would leave its mark on Saint-Sulpice forever! As if by chance a century later, Delacroix chose to paint a *Heliodorus Driven from the Temple*. The story is taken from the Book of the Maccabees, and the scene takes place in the Jerusalem Temple....

The room is vast with light flowing in here and there, giving a false impression of its size. The oblique openings light up what looks like old stage scenery, where the backdrop and bits of sets have been left lying higgledy-piggledy on the floor. There are iron rings set into the walls, beams, pulleys, hoists, counterweights, hooks, bits of plaster. What was the play that was put on in this abandoned space under the roof? The forgotten stage machinery makes one think of a torture chamber or a prison. It gives the impression of something monumental but sad, falling into ruins. This disintegrated world, with its rusty equipment and Harlequin's paraphernalia, is extraordinarily similar to Servandoni's painting. The architect of Saint-Sulpice was a pupil of Panini, the creator of the "imagined view,"[4] and was very influenced by him. Could this be the great illusionist's last trick of all?

Here we have the paradox of the creative artist with many faces, one of the most talented of his day. In scenery design his taste was baroque, but in architecture he was the enemy of profusion and overelaborate style—his great portal at Saint-Sulpice is austere to say the least. There is something of Cagliostro in Servandoni, a side to him that is sometimes like a fairground magician. A tendency to invent a host of characters for himself and play them with such talent must raise suspicion. Let us not forget that he was the inventor of "skewed perspective."

Several people who know the history of Saint-Sulpice have assured me in all seriousness that Servandoni committed suicide by jumping off the north tower, which was still unfinished at that time. This anecdote is repeated over and over. The fact is that his death occurred in the most natural way possible: he died in his bed in 1766. Where does the legend come from? It was no doubt inspired by the dangerous existence of this extravagant, scheming, smooth talker. Servandoni's personality would only encourage the spread of a fable like that.

A moaning sound seems to be coming from a small room covered in dust and facing north. It grows louder, then stops. I turn toward the sacristan.

"That's where the station men used to be," he calmly declares.

"Station men!"

"The telegraph station employees. They used to be in that cubbyhole. You know that there was a telegraph on the top of both towers in the nineteenth century. One was linked to Bayonne and the other to Toulon. Saint-Sulpice was a target for the Prussian artillery during the siege of Paris in 1870 because of these two telegraph lines.

"But what about all that moaning?"

"It's the wind. It blows in through that window. Look, over there!"

Gusts of air pass through the grille in the small windows under the roof, vibrate and whistle, stopping and starting unpredictably. It sometimes sounds like ululation.

"Are there hidden rooms everywhere in this church?"

"You haven't seen anything yet!"

He has stopped walking. Does he mean the remains of colossal plaster moldings in front of him? I hadn't noticed them when I entered the room. I thought they were bits of rubble, but they are actually a jumble of feet, calves, cherubs' heads, urns, and ancient drapery. They are hollow, showing some of the wooden rods used for reinforcement. Now twisted and broken, they look all the more naked and forsaken.

I am looking at the remains of a setting for some eighteenth-century altar, which was intended to give it perspective. Everywhere there is this extraordinary sense of theater, this ability to cast parts in a play, to make a show of itself. The curtain is perpetually going up in Saint-Sulpice. Lafont Saint-James, as early as 1745, accused it of being "the triumph of artistic license and imitation ultramontane style."[5]

"We can go back into the tower now," the sacristan says.

Gusts of wind grab at us as we come out from the area under the roof on to the terrace. Around us, the town is a silver-grey mirage, the still waters of the metal roofs gleaming like wadis. The public squares with their sparse vegetation are oases, the Invalides a dune, its summit shimmering with flame. A vision of the end: dust and silence. One can already foresee the desert of stone in "The holy city set in the west" described by Rimbaud.

"Behind the scenes... You like what goes on behind the scenes? I'm going to show you something that will certainly interest you. Behind the scenes in painting," he said, being deliberately intriguing.

Here is another inscription:

"From the tree that holds us / we fall / never having noticed it."

We have gone back into the tower, deep, dark, and echoing as a well. It is as if we are slowly and heavily making our way into an underground world. The white pieces of paper stuck on the wall of the staircase become more numerous. Who wrote these fragments of poems? These aphorisms with their mannered, elliptical metaphors are sometimes rather like the poetry of René Char.

The sacristan has the knack of selecting the right key from all those on his huge ring. And yet, they all look the same. He stops at a door in the middle of the staircase and thrusts the key into the keyhole.

"This was where the bell ringer lived."

"But this is just like Carhaix's room!"

Carhaix, a character in *Là-Bas*, is the bell ringer of Saint-Sulpice. He lives with his wife in the north tower. The hero, Durtal, likes to visit him and discuss Christian liturgy and the occult sciences.

The room we are entering is very accurately described in Huysmans's novel. I love this book, which has a touch of both holy water and the hair of Beelzebub about it. I was frightened when I read it for the first time in my teens: it gave me a feeling of desecration. Although I believe more than ever in the power of the Prince of Darkness and the spirit of Evil that exists in the world, *Là-Bas* long ago ceased to terrify me. I now find that fin de siècle demonology rather amusing. There are some memorable characters like Mme. Chantelouve, the crazy satanic woman who perverts Durtal, and this good bell ringer Carhaix.

The room has always intrigued me. Huysmans writes of "a dismal room built of hewn stone, vaulted, and lit by a semicircular window just below the ceiling." I always thought that the author had imagined it, but there it is, right in front of me. It hasn't changed. Only the wooden floor, which once was tiled.

How often Durtal dreamed as he looked at that room! He would have loved to set it up to suit his taste and move in there. To be in the clouds above Paris! "To live outside of time at last, while the tide of human stupidity surges against the base of its towers." He talks of "a cosy balmy abode, a warm haven."

A balmy abode! No one but Huysmans would think of expressions like that! I imagine he is referring to the peace and quiet of this refuge, which would soothe sorrows like a balm, rather than of the aromatic smell of the place coming from incense or resin. Today the bell ringer's home smells more of paint, as we have actually entered an artist's studio. White walls, wooden tables, huge stove, tiny flowerpots at the semicircular window. The painter is not in.

I feel as if I have broken into his home and violated the intimacy of his studio. The sacristan reassures me. An angel placed on top of a frame smiles down on me. He is a collage made out of pieces of boxes, which the artist has put together with wire. He has a very knowing look, and seems to be thoroughly familiar with things both visible and invisible. Already in touch with the hereafter, he makes light of the material world.

Why do people always want to know the names of angels? "What is your name?" Jacob asks at the end of the fight. As for the cardboard angel, there is no chance that he will answer. His image wafts through the currents of air that move around the studio. He inhabits that space. One imagines that he is fixed to the panel constructed for him by the artist. Wrong! He escapes. He flies about. He has great fun. The paper angel is a mischievous character.

The sacristan is watching me with some amusement. I have the impression that it is a mise-en-scène staged especially for me. I can't resist telling him.

"A mise-en-scène! Come now!…Just put your trust in Saint-Sulpice," he says gently.

"Where's the painter?"

"It's a woman. She comes here every day."

"Do you mean that she comes into the church to work?"

"Yes…But there's nothing remarkable in that. There are other artists' studios in Saint-Sulpice."

"Other studios! All right. Let's say that it's the usual thing in a church like Saint-Sulpice. And let's admit that the setting, this backstage world with its artists, inaccessible rooms, and forgotten galleries, the whole thing, is frightfully banal. I still need some explanations."

"There's nothing to explain! There's another studio over near the Chapel of the Virgin. A sculptor's studio. And she's a woman too.…"

"What does she sculpt?"

"Angels. Nothing but angels."

"Angels are the specialty of Saint-Sulpice! Where are they still made?"

"Made! Come on, they're artists," he said feigning indignation. "I found two angels when I was tidying up in a cellar in the underground church. From the seventeenth century no less! I'll show them to you. Two marvelous wooden sculptures."

The underground church. I know that the present church was built over an old twelfth-century building. The foundations of Saint-Sulpice rest on a maze of passages, corridors, vaults, and storerooms. I've even come to several plays and a candle-light dinner in one of the rooms in the crypt.

The powerful voice of the organ booms out as we are descending the north tower. Its thundering notes penetrate its wall. The music comes in bursts, almost in circles, as if it were trying to follow the shape of the spiral staircase.

The distant explosion of sound sends a thrill through me. I now understand the excitement felt by Delacroix and his insistence on painting during services in the church. As I step out of the door that gives access to the tower on the ground floor, the warm wave of music envelops me. The empty church has suddenly come to life. The air vibrates.

The angel in the painting with Jacob and the one in *Heliodorus* are dancing, roused into action by the brilliant sunlight shining through the window.

"Did you enjoy seeing what I've shown you?"

"I would never have imagined that such a world could ever exist behind this beautifully ordered exterior. It's extraordinary!" I reply with an enthusiasm that seems to amuse my companion.

"It's the same in all churches. In any house there's an attic, a cellar, a storeroom. One doesn't see them, that's all."

"It's different here. It doesn't give anything away, this church of yours."

"What do you mean?" he asks.

"Well, the clear lines of the building...the nave...Everything seems so transparent, whereas..."

"But we don't hide anything, Monsieur," he says, interrupting me.

"I mean that the back of the picture is as interesting as the front. But there's something I can't put my finger on. I can't work it out. Those studios, those angels...They're all so unexpected!"

"But why complicate things needlessly? You noticed that there's no lack of space here. It's very suitable for artists. And there are also the living quarters."

"Do you mean to say that there are people living in the church?"

"Obviously not in the church itself. There was a hanging garden here for quite some time. Saint-Sulpice is so vast!"

"Well, where are these living quarters?"

"I'm not at liberty to tell you that. One must be discreet, you understand."

"Discreet! You told me a moment ago that there's nothing to hide."

"How can I explain it to you? It's private…. The people concerned don't want it to be known."

"Are they tramps?"

"You must be joking! We do have tramps, but they're at the church door."

"And inside during the day. I know them."

"All of that's a long way from Delacroix!" he says with a sigh and just a hint of reproach.

CHAPTER 2

The Lecturer from the Louvre

"What you see before you is Delacroix's spiritual testament...."

The group of aging middle-class ladies, who determinedly keep in shape with physical workouts and dry courses on painting, suddenly stop talking. Like gym, learning about art later in life is a kind of mortification: it requires concentration and an acceptance of boredom, often mistaken for rigor. There is also something heroic about it, although the practice of group work admittedly offers some compensation. Cultural aerobics, a form of collective exercise, must be carried out against a background of jokes, which unifies the group. It's the thing to find this humorous.

In this case, however, what the woman lecturer leading the group is saying is neither dull nor boring. She is not lacking in eloquence and will sometimes make strong statements when she feels attention waning. The allusion to the "spiritual testament" gets a reaction and communicates a sense of excitement to the group. Members of the little band, who were beginning to disperse in clusters in the middle of the transept, are suddenly welded together again. A spiritual testament on a wall, that's not a common phenomenon, even in a church.

I'm very familiar with that moment. I know it by heart. It's a well-practiced act. She is silent now, like the conductor of an orchestra who insists not only that no one coughs, but also that all eyes, all minds are concentrated on him. The way she does it is naturally less tyrannical: she will appear to sulk to make her little group pay for wandering off.

When I came upon this guided tour, I reacted when I heard the words "spiritual testament" for the first time. She could have said specifically that they originally came from Maurice Barrès. It was only after silencing her followers that she mentioned his name: Barrès, the guardian spirit of the Chapel of the Holy Angels! People find it useful to adopt the ideas of the author of the *Mystère en pleine lumière*.[1] His book is lofty, powerful, and resonant, but certainly questionable on the significance of the scene painted by Delacroix. However, that is not important. The main thing is surely the use a lecturer from the Louvre makes of it? Barrès is a big name that commands respect. The silence she managed to establish and even maintain for several minutes shows that she has awakened the group's curiosity.

Most of them are seeing Delacroix's painting for the first time. Everything conspires to disappoint the newcomer. Intimidated by the huge spaces between the columns of the facade, he or she feels uncertain about entering the church. The door closes with a muffled thud as soon as the visitor crosses the threshold. The somber dulling effect of a tomb, which one feels in places of worship, has no time to manifest itself; besides, Saint-Sulpice does not have that smell of damp cellar, hot wax, and stagnant holy water so typical of our churches.

Could this empty alcove really be Delacroix's chapel? Two panels of twenty-four and a half by nearly sixteen feet. A look of surprise and mainly disillusion comes over people's faces. The energy of *Wrestling with the Angel* does not make an immediate impression. A resistance surrounds the chapel like a frozen charge of electricity, silent but overpowering. Coming face to face with the painting is something of a disappointment: the mind has difficulty in forming an opinion of it or even finding its way into it. Like the caravan Delacroix drew on the wall. It's fascinating the way the procession appears then fades into the distance, only to reappear briefly at the bend of a ravine! This elusive cortege is slowly undermining the wall, cracking it, and eating into it. A sense of confrontation, an absence of tranquillity, still remain in this chapel from the time when the work was taking place, as if the moveable tower of scaffolding the painter used had just been taken down from the wall.

The lecturer had intrigued me the first time I saw her. She also seemed to be looking for something. The demon of curiosity made her nosy, and she looked intently at the faces of her audience as she spoke. When I knew all her little tricks after watching her five or six times, I felt I had to go and speak to her.

I think I can identify nearly all the regular visitors to the chapel, but I don't inevitably make their acquaintance. It would be impossible, and what would be the good of it? I'm not in charge of the visitors' book. I'm not the doorkeeper of the Holy Angels. "Woe betide the writer who says everything there is to say on a subject," Delacroix notes at the end of his *Journal* (a phrase he took from Voltaire). Pride likes to treat everything and forget nothing. Delacroix says time and time again that in painting, as in all the other arts, one must know how to cut down and make sacrifices.

The fifteen or so women who make up the group come and stand behind the lecturer. With their milky flesh, well preserved by antiaging cream and moisturizing balm, their piercing eyes, careful make-up and dark clothes too firmly buttoned up, the assembled company look wan and stiff as they come into the light. The other visitors stop talking. They think they will take advantage of the commentary—people show a sudden interest in anything going on when they realize it is free! But after a few minutes they lose interest in their bargain, become bored, and move on.

Now that she has total silence, the lecturer agrees to speak. She gives another quotation from Barrès, pronouncing the words with a certain amount of emphasis. "Barrès wrote that *Wrestling with the Angel* was 'a final page of autobiography, a summary of the experience of a great life, the last will and testament written by the old artist on the wall of the angels.'"

I very quickly noticed her propensity to hide behind quotations. Barrès and, of course, Baudelaire…On the subject of Delacroix, it is impossible to avoid Baudelaire. And yet his commentary on the Chapel of the Holy Angels is not the most perceptive thing he wrote about him. He is in better form in his defense of the author of *Médée*. A lack of real understanding comes through the obligatory praises.

As it happens, the guide does not quote Baudelaire's article but, as usual, his famous quatrain from *Les Fleurs du mal*:

> Delacroix
> Evil angels haunt this lake of blood
> darkened by the green shade of the firs,
> where under a stricken sky the trumpet-calls
> like a fanfare by Weber fade away.[2]

At that moment the group gets restless and begins to break up. The lecturer is declaiming too much. The straight line of her aquiline nose accentuates the searching, imperious ways she looks at people. She could be considered ugly, but it is an ugliness that, strangely enough, one gets used to: a mixture of ease and authority that is meant to show distinction. Afterward, I could not help pointing out to her that these lines of Baudelaire are not very relevant to the paintings in Saint-Sulpice.

"Can you explain something to me? Where you have seen the 'lake of blood'? Where are the 'evil angels,' 'the firs,' and the 'stricken sky'?"

"There's nothing to explain," she replied with an impertinent smile.

"Then why do you do it?"

"To pad out my talk!" she retorted coldly.

This indifference actually did me a service. It made me look at *Wrestling with the Angel* in a different way. Unbeknown to her— and I'm not even sure if that is the case—she explained Baudelaire's lack of enthusiasm. In the Holy Angels, the poet of *Les Fleurs du mal* failed to find the painter of cruelty and pain he so admired. Baudelaire sees nothing of any value in this religious Delacroix, even though he pretends to admire him. The reason he praises him to the skies is to avoid discussion. Perhaps Baudelaire did not understand the Delacroix of Saint-Sulpice.

The painter writes to the poet to thank him. He is grateful to Baudelaire for having grasped the mysterious effects of line and color, and not opposed the two notions, as is so often the case. Delacroix passes a remark, however, that "those fine fellows the critics only want to understand so that they can prove something." Is that directed at Baudelaire? I've had the feeling from the beginning that this chapel is the grotto of misunderstanding, the holy place of mistakes, the oratory of false pretenses. I find this confusion quite fascinating.

"Deliver me out of the mire, and let me not sink."[3] This is the inscription over the entrance to the Chapel of the Holy Angels.

*   *   *

"Don't you think that the angel in the painting with Jacob has a fantastic body?"

"Fantastic! What do you mean?" The lecturer is surprised, but can't help laughing.

"You know very well what I mean. Stop pointing out all those details about his calves and his thighs in your commentaries! One would think it's all that interests you in the angel. Don't forget he's a celestial being," I tell her pretending to be stern.

She is annoyed. I can tell from the way she hitches her bag up on her shoulder.

"Just what do you disapprove of?"

"I'm trying to understand. You don't seem at all interested in the meaning of the scene!"

"Exegesis is not my field," she replies.

Then she adds in a playful voice,

"Anyway, this chapel is very exciting!"

"Exciting!"

"Yes. There's something very sensual about it."

"Why not say erotic, while you're at it."

"Why not? Have you read *L'Étreinte* [*The Embrace*] by Philippe Vilain?" she asks.

"No."

"Do you know Annie Ernaux?"

"Yes."

"Well, in this novel, the author imagines a love scene with her under this very painting."

"That wouldn't be easy. There are a lot of people coming and going. Unless of course they were very quick...or stayed locked up there all night."

"The author doesn't give any details on that subject," she says with her strange frozen smile that is not without charm.

I find this eroticism rather cheap. Like imitation Huysmans! All those American films about Satanism have corrupted even our lecturers at the Louvre.

She looks angry as she pulls at her shoulder bag, and says sharply, "It just so happens that I've been watching *your* little game for some time too. That indiscreet way you have of prowling around the chapel, watching everything going on there as if you were the keeper! What are you looking for? You're like a cop who wants to arrest us. Why don't you set up an identity check at the entrance?"

"Very funny! So, you take me for a voyeur or a parish fanatic!"

She gives a burst of laughter then resumes that chilly look that gives her a certain chic.

"You take others to be voyeurs. You look at visitors as if it were unhealthy curiosity that draws them to this chapel. If you could see how you stare at them! Others beside yourself have the right to be interested in Delacroix. I can see a lot of vanity in this attitude of yours," she says, having a little dig at me.

She turns her back on me, leaving me standing there in front of *Wrestling with the Angel.*

The angel confronted by Jacob is about to go sprawling. Heliodorus is falling flat on his face. She must think she has made me bite the dust as well. I take a last look at the inscription over the entrance to the chapel: "Deliver me out of the mire, and let me not sink!"

It is easy to get stuck in this corner of Saint-Sulpice—I'm the first to admit it. The further you go, the more you get bogged down.

"Jesus falls for the second time." The chapel is the seventh station of the cross, marking the second time the condemned man falls. Its dominant theme is collapse, defeat, reversal. Stones work loose so that the entrance to the Holy Angels often has to be protected with plastic sheets. The reason for this collapse? The bathroom of the man in charge of the organ bellows has been leaking into the ceiling for decades.

In April 1999, the Entrepose Company finally decided to take down the scaffolding that had been there for years protecting the vault. The stone has been restored but the leak is still there. Now it is the north tower that is wrapped in a gauze bandage kept in place by metal tubes and protected from falling rubble. Work is due to start again shortly.

CHAPTER 3

The Agony and the Ecstasy

In my father's bakery, we hardly spoke of painters, any more than we did of musicians or poets. But we were on good terms with angels. They were everywhere. We kept company with them. They were socially superior to us, but discreet and accommodating. At church we sang hymns in their praise. At the church youth club we imitated them in little plays. As our parish priest was very keen on having this winged presence on the feast of Corpus Christi, we dressed up as members of the celestial band. Each of us also had our own guardian angel. He wept silent tears whenever we did something bad.

Painting seemed a supernatural activity to me when I was young. I first discovered it in the *Petit Larousse*, one of the few books, together with the Jerusalem Bible, that we had in the house. My father was very good at crosswords and was always looking something up in it. The *Larousse* contained reproductions of famous paintings in a hazy sepia brown color. This made them look darker, giving them an abstract and mysterious quality.

My first real encounter with paintings took place in the Rennes Art Museum, which was on the way to my secondary school. I had gone in there one day by chance to kill time as I had missed the showing at the cinema. I particularly liked the place because of the silence and the smell of old leather in the deserted rooms. Strips in the parquet floor moved as you walked over them, making a pleasant, reassuring, woodwork sound. The museum was particularly proud of works by Philippe de Champaigne and La Tour, but the only one to interest me was Rubens and his *Tiger Hunt*, painted for the elector of Bavaria.

I have always stayed faithful to Rubens. Not for his well-endowed females—it is ridiculous to equate him with his fat Flemish women alone—but for the way he painted with such ease. This brio, life itself, comes naturally. To me it seems like a sign of long-lost innocence. I was not aware then that Rubens was Delacroix's favorite painter. Delacroix used his hunting scenes as models for many of his own paintings with wild animals.

I made my acquaintance with Delacroix through my Lagarde and Michard sixth-form school textbook on the nineteenth century. *The Massacre at Chios* was in it. The beautiful torso of the woman on the right tied to the Turkish rider's saddle considerably stirred my senses. I later learned that she was called Émilie Robert. Her talents as a model were not the only thing the artist appreciated about her.

Delacroix, the painter of pleasure and pain. I had not yet understood that these bodies submitting to the fury of cruelty and love were already familiar to me, in fact they were an integral part of my youth. Injury and ecstasy, bestiality and rapture, the fusion of pain and bliss was the very story of the saints, mystics, and martyrs the priests extolled. This threatening religion foretold torture in the next world, but it also offered a triumphant and sensual liturgy. Through its devotion to Mary, "the new Eve," it continually glorified woman; on the other hand, there was constant emphasis on original sin and the wretchedness of fallen man.

What impressed me most about the mystery of the Incarnation was the word *flesh*. Moreover, it was always a question of its "weaknesses" and its "goading." It had to be mortified, which was a huge challenge, the flesh being omnipresent. The words "the work of the flesh" were used to describe the union of man and woman ("Thou shalt not desire the work of the flesh except in marriage" stipulated the ninth commandment). The mystical *body* of Christ, the *body* of the Church—this religion certainly used a lot of physiology even in its most spiritual aspect. Even in the fulfillment of the ultimate purpose, the image of our material substance prevailed once again with the resurrection of the *body*. Where has the soul gone?

We were told repeatedly to subdue our senses. I understood that I had to conquer them and, in fact, to make this a habitual exercise. The wretchedness of man redeemed by love; these were the woes sung about with such joy in hymns taken up by the thundering voice of the organ. To me they seemed like exquisite agony.

My existence was bound by all these prohibitions. The division between Good and Evil was crystal clear. Remorse accompanied sin, confession went with repentance, then finally came the happy end of forgiveness. What other belief could compete with such a merciful religion? Didn't it allow the sinner to fail again and obtain amnesty indefinitely?

In spite of that, was I really prepared for Delacroix? He once wrote: "Man is so bizarre that even in misfortune he can find some form of consolation and almost of pleasure." The creator of *Dante's Boat* repeatedly depicted the first sin, "the universal dog-eat-dog." His paintings present man's savagery; they show his cursed side. Delacroix sizes up the disaster of the world. Through some act of grace, he has also managed to save it from destruction.

Everything was imperceptibly drawing me toward the artist whose painting, as Baudelaire so rightly noted "is like a terrifying hymn to fate and incurable pain." But was this "incurable pain" he portrayed enough to awaken my passionate interest? Perhaps he also made me grasp the fundamental duplicity of evil, which distorts and transforms the world. The original defect continues the work of the Creator. Sin does not always make one guilty: its positive power helps resist the aggression of the world. The Apostle Paul says the same thing: "But where sin abounded, grace did much more abound."[1]

Delacroix obviously did not profess any of that: he painted it. "When I have painted a fine picture, I have not written down a thought. That is what they say. How simple-minded they are," he wrote at the beginning of his career, rebelling against his critics. When he was working on the *Massacre at Chios*, he seemed to prefer "that good black, that blessed dirt" to any other color. A few lines further on he notes, referring to himself: "There is an old leaven, the black depths of an oven to fill."[2] Light and shade, classic and romantic, moderation and excess: Delacroix always lived in the harmony of these opposing claims. They are so symmetrically opposed that it makes them look simplistic. He said of the imagination that it was "the queen of truth," enabling him to reconcile these contradictions so that they became indivisible. They in turn had an energizing effect on him, their mutual resistance acting like a force for order.

This explains why he is sometimes difficult to pin down. He said, for example, that "What is fixed is instability"; he wanted to paint "the flash of a sword." Delacroix is an electric genius: he draws lightning, he fires thunder. It is difficult to describe this energy, this passion brought to the fore by the forces of attraction and repulsion. In Delacroix there is always a controlled impatience, the impression that the matter at hand becomes too weighty and never proceeds quickly enough. In the beginning he was considered a hothead whose brush was described as "a drunken broom." He made himself what he was through this admirably resolved tension.

I can remember the moment when, somewhat stunned by seeing so many fine things, I walked into the Worcester Gallery in the Chicago Art Institute. One of the walls seemed to sparkle as if it were studded with gems. The stones gleamed darkly. This glittering effect could come only from Delacroix: it was the *Battle of the Giaour and Hassan* and a *Lion Hunt*.

The same thing happens every time. I just allow myself to be led by something like an intuition. If a museum has Delacroix paintings, there is no need to point them out to me. Their glow sends out a magnetic field that draws me irresistibly. I go to look at a painting by Delacroix as if I were going to witness a duel. I never tire of seeing this internal struggle. In a talk he gave after the painter's death, Alexandre Dumas remarked that "During his whole life as an artist, Delacroix was what the politicians call an act of war."

These struggles always bring us back to the most difficult challenge of his life. The same magnetic force draws the visitor to *Wrestling with the Angel*. Quite a crowd forms in the chapel sometimes. "Well, what's happening in the picture? But what are the two of them doing?" wonders the curious visitor who has hurried over to see the scene. He then goes away again disappointed, unable to find any meaning in the fight.

When I arrive in a town I have never seen before, I immediately find out if there is a museum. It's an obsession, and I don't really know what I'm looking for. Perhaps the lost smell of the Rennes Art Museum and the Rubens hunting scene. This heady perfume of rancid linseed oil is slightly sour and camphorated, but pleasant. And I know very well that it is the smell of death. All museums have this odor. It has nothing to do with mold or stagnation: it is the smell of departed life or perhaps of blood (Napoleon, who had a highly developed sense of smell, noticed that blood smelled of dust).

"To dust you will return..." This dry, chalky smell, so pleasantly lingering and bland, also has a hint of metal about it. When I go out again after breathing it, my mind always feels emptied—emptied of the ideas it contained before I went in. In this way I have slowly built up a personal, and probably absurd, geography of painting, which owes little to art books and even less to contemporary aesthetics. Why a geography? Why not a zoology? ("And what if it were an animal?") Geography has the advantage of dividing up and classifying. I realized that through successive triangulations I had drawn up my own cartography in which artists, schools, periods, and media formed continents surrounded by oceans, promontories, reefs. Delacroix should logically be a mountain. However, he is a mountain pass: a disturbing place pierced by rays of light.

Jacob Wrestling with the Angel disappears into a pass. The strength of this painting is rooted in the three gigantic trees dominating the scene, but its final destination is situated in the gorge with its misty contours. The convoy of servants, flocks, Jacob's sons and wives will soon disappear into that gully. By the time the first men on horseback go into the narrow entrance, the fight will be over. At the end of the tunnel is the Promised Land.... Everything is frozen at that moment. It belongs to a forbidden, sacred time—a sacred moment because it makes everything last indefinitely. The stream of people and animals in the caravan flows toward the enclosed valley. Delacroix has fixed it in an eternal present.

*   *   *

I knew nothing about painting, but I had the Bible at my finger-tips, an apt expression to describe my habit of flicking it open with my thumb at the right page and then pointing to the required passage. One day at boarding school, the priests confiscated this Jerusalem Bible that my parents had lent me. Direct contact with the Scriptures did not please these men of the Church. They alone had the right to expound it; they alone were authorized to interpret it. All we were allowed was a watered-down version called *Bible History*. At the time I could not understand the reasons for it being forbidden. I thought that these men of the Church—very puritan by the way—wanted to censor the reading of torrid passages from the Song of Songs, which I certainly visited eagerly and often. Like many adolescents of the 1950s, isolated in their villages and curbed by narrow morality, I found many ways of breaking free. The Bible introduced me to sexuality and, above all, to eroticism. As everyone knows, the Old Testament is full of stories about illicit sex, deflowering, onanism, rape, and incest. This violence both frightened and amazed me.

Nevertheless, the Bible for me was a reassuring, perfectly delineated world. I knew my way. I could open it anywhere and still find myself in familiar territory. One verse was enough for me to get my bearings. Genesis began harshly with this demanding God who finally mellowed after seven hundred pages as the New Testament began. It was pointed out to us that what was really important began with Christ.

Bible History, an expurgated version of the Old Testament, endlessly reeled off in catechism class, was considered pure entertainment. Jacob's tricks, Moses's feats, King David's erring ways, the fearlessness of the Maccabees, were told to us like oriental tales, a kind of narration of the *1001 Nights* while waiting for the infant in Bethlehem. But a hidden jealousy, a resentment that dared not speak its name still came through the fantasy in these censored tales. The hero of this extraordinary serial story was certainly the Jewish people whom Yahweh had chosen. Like Scheherazade, they had to hold out until the Gospel of St. Matthew, which began the New Testament.

All these tales held an inner meaning that one had to find for oneself. What was the truth of these stories? What did they mean?

The Bible has a power that compels you. It is not enough just to read it. There comes a moment when the reader has to make the commitment and lift the veil himself. This injunction is no doubt the source of my passion for searching and revealing the truth (and for detective novels). The key to these allegories, the meaning of these stories, the significance of these dramatic events is often obscure and much debated. My experience with the Old and New Testaments has accustomed me to search for the hidden intent, which invariably leads to the sudden revelation of a truth. This need to interpret, born from that biblical imperative, is no gratuitous game: it is a tireless search for proof behind appearances and for going back to the source as far as possible.

The story of Jacob worried me when I was a child. In the beginning, the biblical patriarch and future father of the twelve tribes was nothing but a cheat. His deceit and his trickery were told quite coldly, with almost a hint of admiration. This very strange way he had of stealing his brother Esau's birthright did not seem to sadden the narrator. And the new name for God's chosen people was to have its origin in this crafty devil! One thing really surprised me in this whole story: how could the divine blessing take place since it had been stolen? What was God doing in all of this? He granted this favor, surely he had the power to take it away? I had not yet understood that God had set his creature free. It was the responsibility of each person to seek his salvation or not.

It does not take an expert in biblical exegesis to realize that there is a deep divide separating Jacob's life into two parts: before and after crossing over the Jabbok ford. Before the meeting with the angel there is nothing but tricks and cheating. But the son of Isaac is never the same again after the fight. He bears the mark forever in his flesh. The dislocation of his hip bears witness to his metamorphosis. He is victorious but wounded. This bruising is a sign of his pact with God, the thorn in the flesh the Apostle Paul talks about. For him mutilation is the indelible mark of original sin.

It is not known why Delacroix chose the character of Jacob. On 28 April 1849, the Ministry of the Interior officially commissions him to do the mural paintings for the Font Chapel (its name at that time). The naming of the chapel is significant, and the change will worry the artist. After a lot of thought, he had chosen subjects linked to original sin washed away by the sacrament of baptism.

Delacroix is fifty-one. Louis Napoleon has been president of the Republic for five months. This is no doubt a pleasing state of affairs for the son of Charles Delacroix, a prefect in the First Empire. He has failed at the institute for the fourth time. He is a recognized artist and even admired, but his paintings do not fetch a very good price. He will receive the sum of 26,826 francs for his work on the Chapel of the Holy Angels.

Delacroix is looked upon with some mistrust. He does not fit into any category. He is a false romantic, a true classicist, both worldly and misanthropic, an intimate of the prince-president and a hermit of the Sénart forest. He has an ardent soul and cold, standoffish manners. He is an affluent member of the middle-class with a good head for business, but he leads a sober existence. Indeed, the painter of energy and melancholy has always lived with the clash of opposites. He benefits from this fundamental ambiguity over which he has complete control.

Delacroix has recently begun keeping his *Journal* again after interrupting it in 1824. This diary, a providential but paradoxical undertaking, seems to disclose without actually revealing, as Delacroix is always concealing something at the same time. One often gets lost in the lists of people well-known then but now forgotten. A kind of boredom sometimes emanates from these fierce but petty upper-middle-class prejudices, and the laborious shorthand accounts of emotion too often held in check (especially in the second part). Yet there is nothing more fascinating than this daily report of the artist's thoughts and deeds. In the end one learns little about Delacroix the man: he rarely shows what he is feeling. His self-observation is intended for self-criticism. But what a clear-sighted and penetrating observer of human nature he is! This urbanity is his particular way of mystifying those with whom he comes in contact. Those who can see its infinite nuances appreciate how impertinent it can be.

The decoration of Saint-Sulpice is a project close to his heart. He learns that the chapel, wrongly called the Font Chapel because the baptismal font was temporarily placed there, is dedicated to Saint Sulpice, the patron saint of the parish. On 2 October 1849, it changes name yet again and this time it invokes the Holy Angels. Delacroix is obviously very annoyed by all this. He has the feeling that the parish priest of Saint-Sulpice is creating obstacles for the sake of it. The change of name obliges him to review everything and look for other themes. "The justifiable anger I felt has really knocked me about," he writes.

Bruising and wrath: in a strange way and without being aware of it, he has found the leitmotif of the two paintings that will adorn the chapel. There is the dislocation of Jacob's hip and the fury of the angels beating Heliodorus. The two compositions are an assault against a wall. Even before knowing what he will paint, Delacroix is commencing a battle with a blank, uneven, porous surface. The chapel actually smells of powder. How should he go about occupying it, or more exactly, how should he close in on it and conquer it? He is obsessed by the preparatory work. "For priming the church wall, linseed oil and no other, boiled, lead white and not white zinc, which won't last. Yellow ocher will give the best undercoat" (*Journal*, 8 June 1850).

All he can talk of is rendering and preparation. And the subject? No one has any idea. On 5 October 1850 he finally agrees to reveal his decision. In a letter to a friend, the painter Constant Dutilleux, he mentions not only *Jacob Wrestling with the Angel* and *Heliodorus*, but also the ceiling, which will have as its subject *The Archangel Michael Slaying the Demon*.

There is a passage in the letter that is rather intriguing: "One of the most appealing aspects of religious subjects lies in the fact that they give free rein to the imagination, so that everyone can express his own feeling in them."

He then calls on the imagination and its many and varied representations. The most important thing is to cover one's tracks. In short, as everyone interprets in his own way, it is all the easier for the artist to keep his secret! But what can he have to hide? At that time, he is not aware of it himself. At the very least, he seems to be in no hurry to begin his fight with the wall. From 1850 to 1854 he is preoccupied with another commission, the decoration of the Hall of Peace in the Town Hall, and neglects the Chapel of the Holy Angels.

On 16 June 1854 a major event takes place. On that day Delacroix writes in his *Journal*, "Andrieu has begun work at Saint-Sulpice."

CHAPTER 4

"A trail of light..."

December 1993. I have taken up my position near the pulpit at the beginning of the funeral service. Squalls of wind are hammering between the doors and almost blow out the candles. Sometimes the flame shrinks to a pale filament. When the last trace of incandescence is about to disappear, the wick sizzles, the light grows longer and comes to life again.

The candles in the chapel of the Souls in Purgatory, however, have much less resistance to draughts. Their flames die out and smoke. They turn black and spread through the church a smell redolent of turpentine and the dairy.

I am very fond of this pulpit, a masterpiece of eighteenth-century cabinetmaking. Preachers have deserted it since Vatican II. There could be some doubt about its safety, I must admit: it is only held up by a fragile staircase on each side. Yet the oak canopy broadcasts sound very well and gives the church excellent acoustics. Completed on the eve of the Revolution, the pulpit proved its solidity during the Terror. It was from this rostrum that the parish priest of Saint-Sulpice proclaimed his refusal to accept the civil Constitution of the Clergy. Revolutionary orators often took turns haranguing the mob there.

It was the scene of further verbal conflict during the Commune. One faction, called the Club de la Victoire had chosen Saint-Sulpice as its headquarters. Its most famous figure, Louise

Michel, electrified her faithful followers from this pulpit. In spite of this, Catholic services continued to be celebrated there. The opposing sides confronted each other in song: while one group gave a vigorous rendition of the "Marseillaise," the faithful retaliated by singing the "Parce Domine." On one occasion, there was even the strange sight of two boys occupying the pulpit to announce that God did not exist. The citizen president of the club came next, proclaiming that henceforth there were only two parties in France: the Jesuits and the Democrats. "One of them must disappear, and it is up to the victors to exterminate the vanquished."[1]

"An act of faith and hope," the priest is saying before the assembled company. What act does he mean? The congregation is made up mainly of middle-aged and old men with rather long, brilliantined hair. They are dressed with studied bohemian elegance: astrakhan collars, silk scarves either white or brightly colored, Inverness capes, or cashmere overcoats. The few women in the crowd are wearing toques and muffs. The eccentric touch is more pronounced than the opulence. I notice that the woman lecturer from the Chapel of the Holy Angels is among them. Her clothes clash with the rest of the assembly. She is dressed in black, in what could be described as mortification chic, which is the Yves Saint Laurent Sulpician style. There are few grieving faces, even though it is a funeral service. They seem neither distressed nor unhappy, bored at the very most and certainly dutiful, almost studious. All these dandies fulfilling a duty or acting on a whim look as if they are trying to convince themselves that the ceremony is serious and important.

I have the impression that this church was destined to attract the unusual from the very beginning. *The Atheist's Mass* takes

place in Saint-Sulpice. It was because of this strange title of
Balzac's that I first entered the world of *La Comédie humaine*,
and I have never left it since. There is an extraordinary moment
when the medical student Horace Bianchon is surprised to see
his master, the great surgeon Desplein, a notorious unbeliever,
making his way into the church. He follows him and watches
him hear mass in the Chapel of the Virgin. Bianchon wonders if
he is dreaming. He decides to come back the following year on
the same day at the same time. Sure enough Desplein is there
devoutly following the service. Bianchon then questions the sacristan. The famous doctor has been coming to hear that mass
four times a year for the last twenty years. "He instituted it."
That word has always struck me. What is Desplein's secret?
Balzac, who is very good at orchestrating his effects, reveals it
only at the end.

The funeral service I am attending gives the impression that
the person concerned died a long time ago. No one is in mourning. The faces of the congregation look serious but, on the whole,
hardly despairing.

"We do not wish—any of us—to force Delacroix to reveal his
most intimate secret." There you are. It's for him. One hundred
and thirty years after his death, a mass is still celebrated in his
honor. Such homage would not have displeased this Voltairian;
he was so fond of Catholic pomp and ceremony and had a liking
for the Office for the Dead. As a son of the Age of the Enlightenment, the painter belongs on his father's side to the Republican
bourgeoisie imbued with eighteenth-century skepticism.

"In this church, where he labored and suffered, surrounded by
the prayers of the faithful and the grandiose music of this same
organ, which maestro Georges Schmitt played so splendidly at
that time, in this church where you have come together to pray

and remember him, we commend him, and with him, all your departed friends...."

The priest is referring to the departed members of the *Société nationale des Beaux-Arts*, of which Delacroix was a founder. It was created in 1862 and counted Degas, Maurice Denis, Rodin, Camille Claudel, Fauré, Saint-Saëns among its members. "Whatever the circumstances that may have led him to paint in this church, one may well think it not insignificant that he chose to paint, on two occasions, the struggle between man and God.... "

The organ plays the *Dies irae* that stirred Delacroix so much while he was painting the Chapel of the Holy Angels. The wind blowing under the doors, the flickering flames, the congregation from another age, the solemn melody that the organist embellishes with such skill, all seem to belong to the past rather than the present. They have come to life again in a kind of hallucination, bringing with them the world Delacroix loved. Saint-Sulpice still retains that golden, passionate melancholy the painter experienced when he was working, perched on his scaffolding. The church lends itself to these floating visions. Is it due to the low-tide light? The imagination wanders free in this ebb and flow without ever sinking: the light acts as a source of life and energy. A kind of photosynthesis is at work, metamorphosing the paintings in all the chapels, even the most mediocre of them. The energetic, morbid nineteenth century—that unfashionable province where some men of my generation still like to take refuge. The dull wall of the Holy Angels that needed enlivening, the silence of the confessionals, which makes the slightest sound seem like a din, the great organ...

The organ is an instrument for going back in time. Why does it seem to make time disappear? In the 1950s, I used to work the bellows behind the choir of our parish church. There was no electricity and the wind chambers were activated by a lever that had to be vigorously pulled. I learned much later that the world I lived in still belonged to the nineteenth century—an unchanging, reassuring nineteenth century that had lost the religion of progress somewhere along the line, having probably found it too much of a strain.

I learned to read with a book called *Le Tour de France par deux enfants*. This work of juvenile fiction, which educated generations of French children before and after the 1914 war, was still being used in my village school in the 1950s. We lagged behind, and were neither proud nor ashamed of it. It was no doubt less exhausting to stay with the great inventions from the early years of the century, which the author extolled as promising a glorious future. Children though we were, we knew very well what to believe about what followed. This retroactive illusion probably had some educational value.

The rhythm of life was the same as it had been one hundred years before, based on the ringing of bells, the fair on the feast of Saint Peter, our patron saint, the succession of "moveable and immovable feasts," the forty-hour indulgence that always stopped on the Sunday after the Ascension, the processions, the month of Mary, the sowing and reaping of the crops. I lived in a little village principality south of Rennes. The most important man in it was a portly priest, an excellent Latin scholar. He controlled his flock through fear. We were continually threatened with hell and eternal fire. However, like all good leaders of men, he knew that intimidation alone was not enough. To compensate us for the torture of the damned to come, he displayed a magnificence worthy of the great princes of the Church. The Sunday masses went on forever, but he kept our impatience at bay with a sumptuous liturgy. We were all taken in by it.

Where did our holy man get this inner sense of grandeur? When we came out of church, we all felt slightly stunned. I would get back to the bakery intoxicated by the thunder of the organ, the gold on the chasubles, and the heady smell of the incense. And this does not take into account all the Sunday perfumes that made the atmosphere in the church so pleasantly heavy: the pungent smell of the brilliantine and Pento hair cream worn by the men, and the exotic scents of the carefully turned-out women.

Even if our time on earth was nothing more than a vale of tears, as we were so often told, I did not find our transitory state disagreeable. I have to admit that this pastoral teaching based on fear did traumatize me just a little. But we were all sinners, and far from making me feel guilty, the idea that wrongdoing was universal gave me a feeling of plenitude. I grew up with the idea that God is good. He loves us and forgives us. What a remarkable religion, which tirelessly rescues the guilty. As a child, it seemed to me that the fate of sinners was more enviable than that of the saints. The saints never failed. I was sorry for them. I thought that they got very little out of our short life on earth.

The principles inculcated in us were subject to numerous transgressions. The rules were constantly broken. This no doubt cured me of the haunting sense of absence and emptiness that has marked life at the end of the twentieth century. Paradoxically, my Christian upbringing had hardly prepared me at all for suffering and death.

In his *Journal*, Delacroix wonders if it might be possible to work in the church on Sundays. He would have to get permission from the religious authorities. There are sung masses, and the musical background inspires, even exhilarates him when he is working.

He pursues the subject again a month later. A certain Abbé Coquant objects and proves to be inflexible. Permission is refused. Delacroix goes as far as requesting the emperor and empress to intervene for him. All in vain.

In 1857, when Delacroix is working on the Holy Angels, the voice of the great organ is silenced for the next six years. The instrument was giving up the ghost: the keys, the works, and the pipes were on their last legs. To save Clicquot's masterpiece, an approach was made to the great organ builder of the day, Cavaillé-Coll. He reconstructed it, then completely restored the bellows and the sound equipment, inventing several new systems. The machine was transformed, achieving the magical number of one hundred organ stops, making it the masterpiece of modern organ building.

The artists' chaplain now reminds his audience of all those members who have passed away. The names of Gustave Doré, Foujita, Marquet, Matisse, Rodin, Sisley are mixed with other painters now forgotten. Who was Jean Couy for example? Here they are honored for being deceased rather than for being famous. I love the theatrical and admittedly affected way these names are read out. It is quite a good mixture of ham acting and emotion. Its tone is affected and its expression stiff and sentimental! Perhaps this is our way of stirring the national memory. Pompous speech gives us a thrill. If we want to be touched, we have to declaim.

The chaplain's listing is part of the cult of totems and guardian figures, a remnant of an archaic past that we cherish and invoke as a national lucky charm.

The church of Saint-Sulpice should be one of those lucky monuments to which we attribute a vague beneficent power as vestiges of former splendor. Why is this building where the Marquis de Sade and Baudelaire were baptized always excluded? The national hagiography will not hear a word of it. People prefer the iconic Notre Dame, that enormous patriotic trompe-l'œil with its gargoyles and its Victor Hugo bric-a-brac; French chauvinism's laughing, crying Everyman: *Te Deum* one day and *Miserere* the next. Our impressionable temperament and our tendency to jingoistic hysteria too easily find a home under the arches of Notre Dame.

Saint-Sulpice is so far removed from such high emotion. But this Cartesian country actually hates moderation, and for that reason it rejects Saint-Sulpice's classicism. The architecture is either overpowering or disturbing. On the subject of classicism, the art critic André Chastel spoke of "a specifically French sadness."[2] By emphasizing the virtues of elimination, this style brings out the aspects of deprivation, absence, and emptiness. It seems to show a congenital powerlessness, hence that hard-to-define feeling of melancholy, which is perhaps nothing more than the bitter pleasure of sacrifice.

Saint-Sulpice is a disturbing place. Its aesthetic dictates limits. There is no exuberance, no excess. Anything that has no use is rejected. When removal is considered as amputation, it inspires fear. Yet more than one hundred columns crowd the facade, extending beyond the threshold, and this profusion is not even noticed.

Saint-Sulpice the misfit! In the eighteenth century there were already criticisms of the towers being so strangely distant from each other, disturbing the harmony of the whole. "They overpower the pediment," complained a certain Abbé Gougenot.

Je hais les tours de Saint-Sulpice   I hate the towers of Saint-Sulpice
Quand je les rencontre   Whenever I have seen 'em

| *Je pisse* | I goes and pees |
| *Contre* | Between 'em |

These lines by Raoul Ponchon make this church the laughing stock of all the others in Paris. A plethora of shops selling religious objects and a narrow, domineering clericalism have long made people dislike "the grand chasublery" quarter, as Alfred Jarry called it. It is significant that a generous spirit like Jacques Le Goff, our good-natured ogre of a historian, should balk at this building, like so many others before him. It's inedible, too hard to swallow. "I wonder what I really think of it. Do I want to get myself arrested by the police for offending public morals or don't I feel that compissatory need?"[3]

Is the lack of shadow and mystery to blame? Is it too French? In an article on "The Mystique of Saint-Sulpice,"[4] Henri Ghéon, one of the founders of the *Nouvelle Revue Française*, praised the clarity of this architecture, which is so suited to our character: "There is nothing hidden here under borrowed ornamentation. The central place of worship forms a whole with its pillars and vaults, a readable whole, a logical whole, a radiant whole, an enclosed whole." He compared the great nave to "a Bossuet sermon." That may be so, but who today wants to hear a sermon, even by Bossuet?

And then there is a final complication: Delacroix. Officially he is the pride of this church, its certificate of conformity. Thanks to the Chapel of the Holy Angels, Saint-Sulpice is still relevant to our times, and it is the main reason why tourists come into the church. There is something more: its ambivalence. Saint-Sulpice is both a church and a stage setting: whoever comes through the theatrical entrance has to take part. One is as much an actor as a spectator, as Henri Ghéon observed.

Saint-Sulpice is out of scale. Plans were always too grand, and so much prodigality forced work to cease in 1678 and not resume until 1719. The construction system is enormous; the thickness of the vault, which measures nearly 110 feet at its highest point, is immense. The aisles and the deambulatory are like a huge, almost impassable river winding between the nave and the side chapels.

There is no esplanade in Paris that emphasizes the theatricality of a church as much. Servandoni had wanted to create a large square surrounded by an architectural ensemble. Only one trace of it remains today: a building at the corner of the rue des Canettes, formerly occupied by the publishing house Robert Laffont. The building—where Servandoni died—stands like the last piece of scenery, which would have been the most brilliant stage setting for the church.

The ringing of the bells, dominated by the deep voice of the great bell, announces the end of the service. The congregation is not too unhappy about that; by now they are glad to finish. Nevertheless a group of people linger at the Chapel of the Holy Angels, as if to make the point. The electric lighting is so stark that they cannot admire *Jacob Wrestling with the Angel*. These blinding lights are a disaster.

Darkness fell some time ago, and the candle glow brings out the contours of people's faces. The lecturer is chatting with a slightly decrepit but stylishly dressed dauber who is sporting a loosely tied bow, ostentatiously fluffed out over his thin chest. His silvery hair looks as if it is powdered with frost, turning up nicely at the base of his neck. His gestures have a certain grandiloquence that could look noble. He makes one think of the poet Aragon as portrayed by his wife Elsa.

The golden glow of the lecturer's jewelry softens the severity of her expression and the hardness of her features. Her detached, slightly mocking air can be attractive, but a moment later her face looks fierce. She seems to be cursed with a personality that is demanding and fragile at the same time. It expresses itself in affectation and a melancholy seductive look that can be quite striking. Black, on her, seems almost lewd. The austerity she affects has a disturbing quality, as if this coldness were a sign of something else.

The sacristan, about to close the church, walks purposefully toward the stragglers to make them head toward the exit. His silent authority obliges them to leave.

There is something poignant about the moment when the church empties and falls silent again. The muffled sounds of the town still arrive in waves into this now undefined space with the banging of the vestibule door, and then slowly decrease until the softest modulation suddenly ceases in the solitude of the night. It is the *dying* hour of the day. I am always moved by this shifting moment in the present when everything is about to vanish. All that is left is the light shining in the tabernacle of the Holy Virgin.

If it is true that Saint-Sulpice is no longer completely uninhabited, the mysterious light indicates an absence, an emptiness: the invisible presence disappears for everyone, but, although it can no longer be seen, it is still there in the darkness of the sanctuary.

What happens in a church at night, when all the people have left it? There are certainly no ghostly figures, apart from the Presence, which is no illusory or imaginary manifestation. I see it like the first verses of Genesis, when God created the heaven and the earth and His Spirit "moved upon the face of the waters." This spirit flying over almost nothingness, this divine eye dreaming or lost in an abstraction that will soon come to life, this infinite, slightly grey whiteness that He will darken, this cosmic construct that He already perceives in the chaos: what an extraordinary image.

It takes time for a church to come into existence. In the beginning it is as vast and empty as a desert; it is populated and finally becomes a dense jungle. A lush growth of ex-votos, statues, candelabra, notices, and post-Second Vatican Council material still flourishes there today. These religious plants prosper in the smallest nooks and crannies, turning toward what is dark and hidden, like the reverse of normal plants, which turn to the light. The confined air is heavy with entreaties, black smoke from the candles, trails of incense, and the smell of vestments. One sees certain chapels decline and the altar become bare. The faithful have deserted them, but the damp of devotion and the tears of supplicants leave their trace behind them.

Delacroix confided in his *Journal* that he is very fond of churches: "The fact that they are so old makes them venerable: it is as though they are lined with all the vows that suffering hearts have offered up toward heaven."

"Suffering hearts…" He certainly liked finding them at Saint-Sulpice. One would think that this agnostic believed in the dogma of the communion of saints: the joining together in suffering, as in love, redeems humanity.

"God is in us," he wrote a few months before he died. He adds: "It is this inner presence that makes us admire beauty." In other words, genius is a divine favor. Pity those who are not chosen!

When he is just beginning work on the Chapel of the Holy Angels, he attends the All Souls Day mass with his cousin, the barrister Berryer, in Augerville on 2 November 1854. The Beatitudes make a great impression on him, especially the *Beati pauperes spiritu*, blessed are the poor in spirit. This simplicity of heart was certainly not Delacroix's main virtue. Proud by nature, he was a complex person, always inhibited by the fear of being taken in. "His genius matched our religion perfectly. It is a profoundly sad religion, a religion of universal suffering," Baudelaire notes.

This definition also applies to Saint-Sulpice art. And yet if there was ever a work that showed few Sulpician characteristics, it would be *Jacob Wrestling with the Angel*. The decoration of the other chapels in the church is quite another matter. There one can feel the influence of Ingres, Delacroix's great rival, and especially of his disciples like Mottez, Pichon, and Lafon. Are these "daubers" whom Huysmans despised so much really so awful? The chapels they decorated are in a very bad state, especially in the northern section of the nave where the vaults are stained by leaking rain. Only the frescoes in the Saint Roch Chapel and Delacroix's decorations have been able to be restored as the southern chapels are not affected by rain.

Ingres was almost a neighbor of Delacroix's: at one stage it seemed that he would be given the task of decorating the Chapel of the Souls in Purgatory, the one next to the Holy Angels. Ingres made it a rule never to refuse a commission, but he needed a lot of persuasion to actually do them. In the end the work fell to François-Joseph Heim who was no "dauber," and whose path often crossed that of Delacroix. It was a strange time they spent together at Saint-Sulpice. Heim's painting today is completely burnt, as if *Wrestling with the Angel* had blazed too brightly on the other side of the wall. His work is called *Prayer for the Dead*. One would think there had been a fire in that chapel. It is dedicated to the Souls in Purgatory and is as dark in there as in hell.

To add to the lugubrious atmosphere, Heim on the other wall depicted *Religion Exhorting the Christian to Suffer*. You have to strain your eyes when you look at it, for there is not much left to see, nothing more than shadows, some grey figures, bits and pieces of the background. Clesinger's *Pietà* stuck up against the stained-glass window has obscured everything. He is largely responsible for the dismal atmosphere in this oratory. Clesinger was George Sand's son-in-law. According to the sharp-tongued Delacroix, he was a boor.

By the time Delacroix begins, Heim has long ago finished his work on the neighboring chapel. There is no mention of colleagues in the *Journal*, no impression of Saint-Sulpice, its architecture or its atmosphere. It is of no importance at all to him. He works away in his corner and the only other thing that interests him is the organ, or more accurately, the harmony it produces.

The memorial service I have just attended makes me think of François Mauriac's affection for the church. This is how he describes Francis Poulenc's funeral in a passage from his *Notebooks*: "I quietly thought of him in this church of Saint-Sulpice, which Huysmans taught us to see as ugly when I was young, and which I've always liked and today like best of all the churches in Paris." It is amazing how Mauriac associates Poulenc's music with Saint-Sulpice. "Like Sulpician architecture, it is more continuation than innovation [...] everything is composed with great spirituality, but also with a charm, grace, and lightheartedness that is basically a form of modesty."

Mauriac mentions lightheartedness in connection with Saint-Sulpice. He is the only one to have seen "the Servandoni side," a look that can be ostentatious and light at the same time; there is freedom and fluidity but also restraint. The same ostentation tempered by irony is present in *Jacob Wrestling with the Angel*: the angel, with a mocking look on his face, holds rash Jacob at a distance.

Another passage in the *Notebook* concerning Saint-Sulpice reminds me of the memorial service for Delacroix. Mauriac describes the funeral of his tutor, Monsieur Carreyre, a priest who was also his philosophy teacher at the Grand-Lebrun College in Bordeaux. "Looking at the old Sulpician lying there, I think how he had heard the cicadas of my youth, breathed the marshy smell of the stream during those bright nights so long ago." Nothing is more moving to me than that scene: the open coffin of the old teacher on its raised platform in the main transept, and the feeling of happiness inspired by the memory of the cicadas at Saint-Symphorien. I often go and listen to their song. My house in the Landes is very close to the old Mauriac family home by the waters of the Hure, just a stream really, but after reading *The Frontenac Mystery*, it seems as majestic as a river.

Everything ends in Saint-Sulpice. The lush summer evenings with the smell of warm resin...But nothing is lost; their scent still lingers. There is something of them in the Chapel of the Virgin: wafts of burnt incense and wax, as if all the perfumes of the church come together in the choir to intoxicate us, and then fade away. Mauriac nevertheless found the Virgin in the chapel sculpted by Pigalle, "not very good at all."

As far as the faithful are concerned, the Chapel of the Virgin seems to overshadow the Holy Angels—it is certainly more strategically placed than Delacroix's draughty chapel near the entrance. I hold it against Mauriac just a little for neglecting the Holy Angels. He wrote so well of Delacroix elsewhere when he referred to the "three rivers of fire" that run through what he calls the painter's "empire": *libido sentiendi, libido sciendi, libido dominandi* (the desire to feel, the desire to know, and the desire to dominate).

A flash of light falls across the Chapel of the Holy Angels. The entrance door bangs. The sad, dull sound disintegrates into the night. That's it! The church is now under lock and key. A new life begins. The rumbling sound from the double doors can still be heard; it reverberates one last time under the arches.

In the midst of darkness, Saint-Sulpice shines from every facet. This shimmering light comes through the windows in the chapels, illuminated by the floodlights outside, making the church sparkle in the night like a black diamond.

On 16 June 1948, lightning fell on the conductor mounted on the south tower. The architect from Historic Monuments noted in his report that "a trail of light ran through the inside of the church right up to the lamp on the altar."

CHAPTER 5

The Dieppe Hotel

"Andrieu has begun work at Saint-Sulpice." On 16 June 1854 one of the most unusual artistic adventures of the Second Empire begins. Pierre Andrieu was a pupil of Delacroix before becoming his collaborator from 1850 onwards.

One of his diaries was found twenty years ago. From 1852–53, the assistant had written down the master's directions concerning technique and color. These notes indicate that from the very beginning Delacroix had a very clear idea not only about the scenes to be depicted—it was later that he lost his way—but also about nuances and tones:

> Jacob
>> Sky   towards the top Prussian blue
>> and white—violet tones umber [*terre d'ombre*]

These instructions have an elliptical beauty whose conciseness seems to associate two realities: the profession, and above all a hidden enigma suggested by images and colors. These disconnected, unpunctuated phrases, taken down as the master dictated them, are a blend of prosaic details and incantatory expressions that make one think of Mallarmé ("Angel, shadow of the flesh" [*Ange, ombre de la chair*]).

Pierre Andrieu was the faithful companion of Delacroix's last years. Could he have been "the rascal" who had no hesitation in attributing his own sketches to the master after his death, as was suggested? Delacroix had confidence in his "junior clerk" and happily relied on him at the preparatory stage.

Andrieu is the main witness. He could see what no one else has seen. Delacroix let him know the nature of the undertaking without, however, revealing details of the content. Shut away in the chapel closed to the public for years, Andrieu, who is both spectator and participant, bit by bit delivers a message that he does not understand.

On 25 June Delacroix writes: "I have been to Saint-Sulpice to see what Andrieu has marked out. Everything works together wonderfully and I think that all will go very well. An excellent beginning." After that, the work done by Andrieu, the initiate kept in ignorance, will consist of squaring off the sketches, putting them on the wall, painting the grisaille, and deepening the colors.

Delacroix always feels a thrill at the beginning of a project. As soon as he comes through the door of Saint-Sulpice, he feels elated. "My heart beats faster when I am in the presence of large walls to be painted" (30 June).

Walls. He talks about them as if he were surrounded by mines or engines of war. In addition to the martial metaphors, he likes a wager and the challenge of a difficulty to be overcome. He has never given the impression that there is so much at stake with his other paintings, not even *The Death of Sardanapalus*. What does he have to win—or to lose—in this undertaking? He says nothing about that. The work is more important to him than anything else.

While he is working at Saint-Sulpice, he wonders in his *Journal* about "this strange need for solitude, which seems so much at odds with a tendency toward exaggerated benevolence." He admits to being "nervy and irritable," but analyzes this contradiction very well. "I want to please a workman who brings me a piece of furniture; if I meet a man by chance, I want him to go away satisfied, be he a peasant or a man of high rank"(1 July 1854). This desperate need to please reveals a man who must be loved at all costs. Deep down, this cold, arrogant dandy is not very sure of himself. More than anything else he wants to present the image of perfection to others, but he is continually haunted by sexual impotence. An anxious soul, forever analyzing himself, he is afraid of disappointing people, while despising himself for harboring such a weakness. These outpourings do not occur very often in his writings. They do happen, strangely enough, when he begins the work at Saint-Sulpice.

Two weeks later, he stops working and leaves for Dieppe with Jenny Le Guillou. They stay at the Hôtel du Géant, then at number 6 Quai Duquesne. She has been his servant since 1835. She is ugly, rude, and totally devoted. Delacroix is fond of this simple soul and likes to take her with him on his outings, but she was never his mistress, contrary to a rumor spread by one of the painter's pupils. He wanted her to accompany him to Dieppe, not to serve him, but to regain her health, which he reports as being "very bad." (Baudelaire maintains that one day in the Louvre, he came across Delacroix explaining the mysteries of Assyrian sculpture to his old servant.)

Saint-Sulpice is left unfinished. It will not be the first or the last time. He needs to look at the sea to reflect, observe, and feel. He watches the boats, calculates the tides, scans the movement of the sky and the shadows on the sea. He takes everything down in his notebook. He is also bored.

After staying in Dieppe for five weeks in the company of his housekeeper, he comes back to Paris. In the evening he dines at

Véry's, the fashionable restaurateur: "The wine there is worse than in Dieppe."

Literature, music, or metaphysics are not the only things that interest him. "Eugène Delacroix was a man of great general knowledge as well as a painter devoted to his art," Baudelaire records. The *Journal* is dotted with comments about gastronomy, wine, the art of the cigar. On those subjects, the great man grumbles a good deal. He complains that the standard of cuisine is falling, that Bordeaux wine is too expensive. A bad Havana cigar actually hindered his inspiration! "Digestion, the vile thing, is the great arbiter of our feelings," he notes prosaically, rather unusually for him.

On the subject of his feelings, Delacroix remains always discreet. The date of 2 October 1854, when he attacks the wall in the Holy Angels, is very revealing. On coming home from Véry's, he writes in the *Journal*: "Apart from one person in the world who is close to my heart, the rest weary me quickly and disappear without trace." Who then is this person who finds favor in his heart? He does not mention her name, but we know that it is Jenny the servant, his "bodyguard."

The painter never married. "The supreme affliction of life is the inevitable solitude to which the heart is condemned. A wife who is your equal is the greatest possession there is. I would prefer her to be superior to me in every way, rather than the opposite," he wrote as early as 1823. He was twenty-five.

It is easy to find evidence in the *Journal* of his taste for models and love affairs with servants. In his youth he would use puerile circumlocutions for the sexual act: for example the Italian *chiavatura* (turn of the key, plus the number, which was never more than two). Interesting the use of this word meaning closure to name intercourse. Love—a kind of shutting oneself away. He locks himself in well before Saint-Sulpice. "I'll need a mistress to subdue the habit of the flesh," he noted at that time.

The habit of the flesh! An apt expression for that sensuality one must overcome. But, in his young experimental days, Delacroix was not always the restrained person the Saint-Sulpice paintings might suggest. In a letter to Stendhal in 1831, Mérimée describes an orgy with "six girls *in naturalibus*": "Your friend Delacroix was wild. He was breathless, panting and wanted to screw all of them at once. If it were not for the respect one owes to the writing paper, I could tell you some strange things about his erotic enthusiasm." It's actually quite difficult to imagine him having a wild time.

There is one woman among those Delacroix loved who stands out because of her marvelous name: Alberthe de Rubempré. Was Balzac thinking of her when he wrote *Illusions perdues*? (Incidentally, it was a bishop named Rastignac who consecrated the church of Saint-Sulpice when it was finally finished in 1745.) Poupillier, the hero of *Les Petits-Bourgeois*, Balzac's last, unfinished novel, is a verger at Saint-Sulpice.

I really like the Christian name Alberthe, especially the rather germanic *h*, which is elegantly excessive like a piece of costume jewelry. She adored trinkets, by the way. It was not a name for a handsome woman or a demimondaine. Alberthe was her real name, and she had married a Count de Rubempré. She was a distant cousin of Delacroix's, and also the mistress of Stendhal and Mérimée. Such a prestigious trio merits our admiration. "She is a very extraordinary woman, pretty, very witty, and on bad terms with her husband. She is only twenty-four. What is more, she shows great frankness and can talk about anything like a man," Mérimée writes.

Delacroix sees her again thirty-four years later at the time when he is working on the Chapel of the Holy Angels. "I've been to see dear Alberthe, whom I found rather subdued in her big alchemist's chamber. She was wearing some of those weird clothes that make her look like a sorceress. She always liked this necromancy business, even at the time when her real magic was her beauty." A comment tinged with a melancholy that is detached to say the least, and so typical of Delacroix. One day Alberthe decides to come to the chapel and surprise her former lover, but soon gives up the idea in case she might be in the way.

He is fifty-five at that stage, and no longer a man to feel much pity. Impulses of the heart weary him. His head is elsewhere. He stopped engaging in light-hearted gallantries ages ago. He still maintains affectionate ties with Joséphine de Forget, his longest-lasting relationship, begun in 1834. The daughter of Lavalette, the hero of a famous escape under the Restoration,[1] this Joséphine is another of Delacroix's cousins—he has an incredible number of them! He calls her "The Consoler," which is only half flattering for her. She soothes, diverts, relieves, and comforts, but that is about all. In his letters he calls her "My kind darling." Delacroix needs this coquette to give him something else to think about. She goes to the salons; he, the loner, adores hearing her gossip. Like many misanthropic men, he is very curious about other people: the human menagerie is a great subject for observation. "Your letters are still one of the main distractions of my life here," he writes.

Here refers to Champrosay, the house close to Paris where he loves to get away. Situated on the edge of the Sénart forest, this retreat is of major importance in the work and conception of *Jacob Wrestling with the Angel*. He often leaves Champrosay in the morning, catches the train at Ris station to go to Saint-

Sulpice, then comes back in the evening to sleep in his hermitage, which he prizes above everything else.

In this month of October 1854, he is determined to devote himself seriously to *Wrestling with the Angel*. The enthusiasm he showed on his return from Dieppe quickly faded. He has still not resolved the problem of preparing the wall. He sent an urgent letter in June to Victor Baltard, the director of Works for Paris and the Department of the Seine: "Allow me to insist on the necessity for the various coats I requested for the walls: even if you put on a much larger number, I am sure you would not prevent absorption." He is obsessed by absorption. A painter's hard work can disappear into a wall that greedily swallows up the slightest liquid preparation.

Delacroix is in battle mode, as if he were besieging a castle. He often uses the word *muraille*, meaning a town wall or high wall, rather than *mur*, the more general term and usually used for an interior wall. During the many long years he spends at Saint-Sulpice, the chapel will become an entrenched camp, a prison. And it will be closed off by a palisade. The painter barricades himself behind it, the better to take possession of the rampart, which seems to elude him. He will spend ten years working on the approach and seven years scaling the east and west sides of the chapel. He will fall several times. Why is he so determined to finish it? He becomes ill and will be on the verge of giving up several times. When everything is ready, and he is about to make his victorious assault in 1860, he confesses to his cousin, the barrister Berryer, that it is: "A work that has become the nightmare of my days and which I'll probably never finish." He chose that prison himself. Now he comes to loathe it.

"The great enemy is the dampness of the walls: in short, the walls are dreadful for any paint. Oil, sinking in to a great depth, can compensate for the drawback." Always this fear of being submerged, swallowed up!

He has hardly arrived in Paris before he sets off to spend two weeks with Berryer in his château at Augerville. This château, near Malesherbes, also played a major role in Delacroix's life, particularly when he was working at Saint-Sulpice.

Berryer, the legitimist[2] orator and well-known figure of the royalist opposition, defended Prince Louis Napoleon in 1840, after the Boulogne coup. Barbey d'Aurevilly called him "the old actress of the legitimacy." He was theatrical, something of a show-off, a womanizer, and rather likeable. He bought Augerville in 1825. It is a Renaissance château, which once belonged to Jacques Cœur, Charles VII's silversmith. Delacroix enjoys this retreat. Being a very "couth" individual, it suits his temperament. He can enjoy both social life and solitude there. He had come in May, and enjoyed making a few sketches of the château. Chateaubriand, Musset, and Lacordaire had stayed at Augerville in the past.

Delacroix is fascinated by the ceiling in his bedroom, which is decorated with a fresco of the Great Condé on horseback at the time of the Fronde.[3] "These paintings are amazingly fresh. The accentuated gilding hasn't been affected at all," he comments enthusiastically. Berryer, who is a great practical joker, is delighted by the trick he has played on his cousin. The fresco is, in fact, the work of a contemporary of Delacroix, who had fun painting a pastiche of seventeenth-century style.

The social gatherings amuse but also irritate him. He complains that life at the château prevents him from working: "Only solitude, and being secure in solitude, allows one to undertake and finish a project." The *Journal* gives ample account of the vexations he feels at this time: "I feel very isolated, and this situation worries me still more for the future....I like a lot of people whom I'm pleased to see, but they have to arrive at the right moment." Among the frequent visitors at Augerville is one of Berryer's cousins, Mme. Jaubert, who wrote a book of memoirs called *Souvenirs*, published in 1881. She is the source of the legend that Talleyrand was Delacroix's father. This rumor, spread about after Delacroix's death, does not seem to have been given much credence in his lifetime.

Saint-Sulpice will once again be left unfinished. Delacroix will not begin again until ten months later, in July 1855. The work is not progressing. Other tasks are taking up too much of his time. He is an artist who loves his labor above all else, and is scrupulous about it. But the punishing schedule he had taken on does not explain everything. He is avoiding the moment of truth. He has doubts. The subject is escaping him. In short, he is afraid.

Dieppe. Number 6 Quai Duquesne. September 1994. Delacroix's address is now a café called Le Chalut. Drinkers are smoking at the bar, looking as if their minds are far away. The place has a sour smell of *croque-monsieur* mixed with the acrid smoke of dark tobacco cigarettes. The owner has no idea that Delacroix stayed on the first floor.

"He's a painter," I tell him.

"Is he famous?"

"Remember?" a customer butts in, "He was the one on the one hundred-franc note."

"You have to be someone to get on a banknote!" the owner declares.

His gestures, which had been quick up to this point, now become very slow. He puts the empty glasses down on the bar very gently, and a crafty, knowing look comes into his eyes. He seems preoccupied. He is thinking, "Perhaps there's a little gold mine waiting up there on the first floor."

"So, he's a painter! In that case, I'm going to take the wallpaper off the first floor."

Where on earth had he got hold of the story about wallpaper? From television, of course. He tells me about a hotel in Brittany where paintings "worth a fortune" had been found behind the paper. I finally realize that it's the Henry house at Le Pouldu. Gauguin and other artists of the Pont-Aven school had boarded there.

"You're not going to start upping the drink prices!" a customer exclaims.

As I'm paying, the owner looks at me anxiously and whispers, "You're quite sure it's number 6?"

Now everyone in the café is talking. Their voices become louder, and I can sense a quarrel in the air. All because a century and a half ago Delacroix rented the first floor. Is that glory? Delacroix said that it was not "an empty word" for him. "It comes from real happiness," he wrote.

I can feel this excitement rippling like water. There is something heady and vaguely indecent about it.

CHAPTER 6

The Café de la Mairie

> "If you can't see Delacroix pushing the paint with
> his brush, you haven't understood anything about
> this painting."

The art critic talking to me is a friend. Léopold introduced me to *Jacob Wrestling with the Angel* at the beginning of the 1980s. He has forgotten about it and I'm not about to refresh his memory, as he would just tell me how shrewd he was. This is quite true all the same. He has the knack of being able to match each of his friends with a work of art or a book according to the particular sensibility he perceives in them. Léopold is not really boastful or fanatical. An ace at concepts and a champion at abstract ideas, he can tease out their intricacies with remarkable dexterity, adding a detail or an observation to his explanation so convincingly that his amazing theories always seem authentic. He hates simple definitions, vague truths, obvious comparisons; he reveres paradox, double meaning, implication.

I've known him since the end of the 1970s, when he was working for an art journal. His florid complexion shows him to be a lover of good wine, and he has nice hands like those of a jolly prelate. He always appears in black and an elegant felt hat with an enormous flat bow.

I can remember the day when it all began. We were sitting on the terrace of the Café de la Mairie in the Place Saint-Sulpice. I was listening to his discourse on Georges Perec's *Tentative d'épuisement d'un lieu parisien*, which had been published a few years earlier.[1] Wherever we may be, Léopold finds a link with a literary authority, an artist, or a historical event. With him, everything is a source of reference to something else. Even with the most vulgar, trivial things, he manages to produce a principle or an anecdote. He is the king of verbal annotation, but instead of expressing it in writing as a footnote, he expounds it orally with continual parentheses. When he does write, his verve and agility of mind never wander from the point. He has a genius for clarity plus the gift of popularization. He talks to me incessantly about "the multimedia revolution," and how France is "lagging behind." Modernity is his key word, his supreme imperative, his obsession. "Really serious things in painting began with Cézanne," he keeps asserting vehemently, waving his manicured hands in the air.

Perec's text is a kind of inventory. Sitting on the same terrace as we were then, the writer scrupulously described everything one usually does not notice: the eighty-six bus on its way to Montparnasse station, an old man passing by with his half-baguette, a basset hound, string tied around the trunk of a tree, the bells of Saint-Sulpice church. A strange and vivid poetry evoking the hidden soul of a square in Paris slowly emerges from this seemingly unimportant accumulation of detail.

"Just think of it! Describing what is happening when nothing is happening at all...Details one couldn't care less about. That's what is so fascinating. Literature today can't do that any more."

He was pleased that the square had held out against the invasion by luxury shops. The big names in fashion, watches, and jewelry from the Right Bank may have wormed their way into the neighboring streets; Saint-Sulpice stands firm. But for how long? The little esplanade still has the look of a provincial public square. The Visconti Fountain is decorated with lions and prelates, and in summer the grotesque masks spouting water babble to the lovers. Lots of coins are thrown into the water. Léopold likes to say that people think they are in Rome.

The bells of Saint-Sulpice start chiming as they do in Perec.

"Have you noticed how far apart the towers are? It's a very original idea! The southern tower is unfinished. Look at all those holes...."

"The birds have probably hollowed them out for their nests."

"Birds! With their beaks perhaps! No, it's from the scaffolding that used to be there. Holes were made in the tower to support the platforms and ramps. They're called putlog holes. The put- logs have never been filled up again. They're strange, these two towers. Victor Hugo compared them to two clarinets. That's fairly accurate. Look at the openings. Just like finger holes. Of course you know the church of Saint-Sulpice...."

As you may imagine, my friend said this "of course" with no real conviction at all. He had guessed that I'd never been inside it.

"Sulpician style doesn't really...," I replied.

"Sulpician! Sulpician! That's silly! There's actually nothing Sulpician about it. You've just never bothered to look at it. Let's go!" he said happily rubbing his hands. "I'll show you something that will really please you."

He knew the church by heart. I remember the short, soft thump of the door after we entered—the inimitable sound of Saint-Sulpice! I remember the first impression of the soft, lumi- nous interior, the filtered half-light, and then Delacroix appear- ing all at once out of the twilight.... It was dazzling to come upon the chapel, which suddenly presents itself without warn- ing, almost like a false note in the dim light.

I was immediately aware that Delacroix's painting *clashed* with its surroundings. But it was not this dissonance that attracted my attention. I only had eyes for *Wrestling with the Angel*. God knows I distrust those chance meetings or revelations that are supposed to totally change someone's life, like Saint Augustine in the garden in Milan ("*Rupisti surditatem meam*," a barrier of deafness fell) or the revelation at Tournon when Mallarmé was suddenly purified by the darkness of the night.

At the time I didn't realize that this painting would cloud my eyes rather than open them. This wall clearly harbored a hidden meaning.

Léopold had the self-satisfied look of a person who thinks he owns something. The initiator always thinks he is the inventor of the idea he is presenting. In a way he was, and remained so. For a long time I was unable to dissociate that painting from Léopold himself.

I was only half listening to what he was saying, catching a few words here and there: "The angel's robe, the blue grey..." At the time I failed to notice an obvious fact: he didn't like *Wrestling with the Angel*. The only element to win his approval was the pile of clothes left in the foreground by Jacob. "Those intertwining touches, that energetic crosshatching: now that's modern! Delacroix is revealing his technique, he shows it off, he's criticizing himself. As for the rest..."

On looking back, I was more intrigued than genuinely interested. I was surprised to find Delacroix in this church. I was fascinated by the angel's big calf muscles. Something inelegant and stiff in his stance seemed to give the whole figure a rudimentary, awkward look. I was looking at *Wrestling with the Angel*, but it was the church that interested me. There was an element disturbing the harmony, but which one? I liked the building straight away in spite of its dirty walls—the dull grey has a miraculous ability to catch the light. In the days and weeks that followed, I surprised myself thinking about the chapel. It was not an obsession: just an impression that was slowly instilling itself into my mind; hardly even an image. But the vision was quietly working within me, without my being aware of it.

One day I arranged to meet Léopold at the Café de la Mairie with the idea of taking him into Saint-Sulpice. I don't know why, but I felt I had to hide my intention from him. Perhaps the painting had already come to mean something to me. Besides, how could I explain the reasons to him when I couldn't work them out myself?

"Why don't we go and see the church!" This was the way we always ended our conversations. My friend asked for nothing better. It was an opportunity to display his erudition. I have to say in all honesty that he has taught me a lot. Above all, how to look at things. How many times has he told me: "You must never tell the story of a painting. It's the worst thing you can do. A painting doesn't tell a story; it produces energy. Yes, it's energy that has been enclosed in a frame, in a rectangle."

He had a thermodynamic approach to painting: fire and strength, incandescence and movement, which is fairly appropriate for Delacroix. Have I really learned his lessons? The tourists certainly loved them. First of all they would stop in astonishment. Their faces showed obvious disapproval or irony at the spectacle of such a conceited talker. Then the miracle happened. Just as they were about to leave, a word, a phrase or a detail would hold them back. My guide enjoyed this power, not without a touch of pride.

But it was a game, an affectation that he exaggerated so as not to be taken in by it. Overacting to avoid making a fool of himself.

Besides, when there were too many people around him, he would put them off the track by leading me into another chapel. Quite a lot followed us, advancing timidly in little clusters. Léopold did not dare turn away his latest fans. "All the same, I can't just send them packing. You've noticed. There are some foreigners among them.... The honor of France is at stake here." He could not have cared less about the honor of France.

He usually led us into Saint Roch's Chapel. It was decorated in 1822 by one Abel de Pujol, a pupil of David. It still looks unfinished even today, perhaps because of the small number of ex-votos, which leave a lot of blank space on the wall. One suspects that Saint Roch may not have granted many prayers.

My companion was fulsome in his praise of Abel de Pujol, a painter now all but forgotten. How often has he bored me stiff with the art of the fresco, a procedure, as everyone knows, which uses watercolor on a coat of damp lime! "Painting wet, *fresco* in Italian, you know!"

There is nothing I don't know now about *intonaco*, the top layer of the coat that absorbs the colors. "It must be done quickly, as the colors don't stay on the surface; they sink into the wall. The lime dries and crystallizes on contact with the air. At least Pujol tried to do it. Delacroix didn't risk it. It must be said that he had had a bad experience at Valmont Abbey."

At the time I swallowed everything he said without checking it. My friend embroidered on the truth, bitten by that form of intellectual games-playing that the Italians call *bravura*, the desire to extend the truth, to overdo the point to keep people's attention. Later, when I decided to follow the track of Delacroix, I wanted to go the Valmont Abbey, near Fécamp.

Valmont was very important to him. The property belonged to his cousins Bataille and Bornot—cousins are an essential link in

Delacroix's life, if only because they determined most of his trips. I saw the Valmont frescoes above a door in the corridor shortly before they were taken off the abbey wall and sent to the Delacroix Museum. For the first time since the Revolution the monastery is once again occupied by nuns.

In reality, Delacroix's attempt at fresco in 1834 was not unsuccessful at all. It consists of three mythological scenes in a fresh, naïve Pompeian style. And it is not the difficulty of the process that the painter seems to have later found disagreeable. Quite the contrary. He even states that fresco is not complicated "materially speaking," and that it is wrong to think that there is no possibility of touching up. In his opinion it is a rather primitive genre belonging to a time when the secret of oil painting has not been discovered. Delacroix adds: "Fresco becomes more and more dull and pale with time."

I must admit I did not notice the effects of time when my friend was giving me his commentary on Abel de Pujol's fresco. There was not much left to see as the damp had etched its own motifs, which dominated the scenes painted by his dear Abel. Léopold took this into account and spoke of "a fascinating palimpsest." Abbé Lemesle, the priest at Saint-Sulpice, was already predicting in 1931 that "These frescoes will inevitably disappear in a very short time."[2] The abnormal distortion of the faces has disappeared since the frescoes have been restored. Not before time.

I miss the original version. The cold muted colors and the vaguely indecent poses of the figures reminded me of Balthus's paintings. I realized later that Abel de Pujol was not the obscure artist my friend wanted me to believe. This pupil of David was very successful in his lifetime. At the time when Delacroix was decorating the library of the Assemblée Nationale, Abel de Pujol,

a member of the institute, had already painted the ceiling of the
Salle des Distributions in the same building. Like Delacroix, he
had worked on the Louvre and the Palais du Luxembourg. Both
of them can also be found in Saint-Denis-du-Saint-Sacrement.

There is another interesting feature that Léopold liked to
explain: a long copper rod embedded in the floor of the church,
which he showed me one day, asking me to guess why it was
there. He loved to play the schoolmaster and thought that a stu-
pid reply could serve an eminently pedagogical purpose.

The copper strip begins at a marble square set into the floor of
the southern transept, continues behind the communion table,
and ends at a white marble obelisk against the wall in the northern arm of the transept. I went up to look at the needle-shaped
column. On the top is a ball surmounted by a cross. The answer
to the puzzle is written on the base of the obelisk:

"*Gnomon astronomicus.*"

"*Gnomon?* But that's Greek!"

"It also exists in French. It's an astronomical instrument. See
that window?"

He pointed to the upper window in the southern arm of the
transept.

"There are two little holes on the right. It's actually a lens. At
midday a ray of sunlight passing through it strikes the copper
band exactly. That line is actually the meridian. It's essential for
understanding *Wrestling with the Angel*. The Chapel of the Holy
Angels faces south. Delacroix played with that light flowing in
directly through the window. Saint-Sulpice cannot be understood without this. This is a very unusual concept for a church:
it's solar architecture. Heliotropism is not the strong point of
Christian churches; they usually seek the dark and somber. The
cult of the sun is a pagan thing: Ra, Phoebus... Anything that

comes from the sun is a bit suspicious. Look around you! Everything in architecture that obstructs light—colored windows, buttresses, high roofing—all that has been done away with. This gnomon is a rarity in a church. It really defines the building. The idea came from an eighteenth-century priest of Saint-Sulpice who wanted to make the ecclesiastical computation absolutely accurate."

"The computation?"

"You know. The calculation! Used to draw up the calendar of moveable feasts. So you can work out the March equinox and Easter Sunday, which, as you know, change every year. And the computation contains the golden number."

"It is thus, Lord, that Thou hast given a limit to our days and all our life is nothing in thine eyes."

"What are you talking about?"

"I'm reading what's written on the obelisk."

The inscription looks as if it has been erased in places. I learned later that this was the work of the Revolution, which had ordered all allusions to King Louis XV to be hammered out. It was under his reign that the gnomon had been installed. In 1792 the church had become a place for public meetings. The Luxembourg *section* had installed an office to enroll volunteers in the Chapel of the Sacred Heart. The execution of the Carmelite prisoners during the September massacres was decided during one of these assemblies. In the following year, the church was dedicated to the worship of the Goddess Reason.

During these visits, my guide always disregarded the Chapel of the Souls in Purgatory. He who was so eloquent on the subject of Abel de Pujol or the other artists of Saint-Sulpice, omitted the painting of François-Joseph Heim, Delacroix's neighbor.

"You can't see anything, and anyway, there's nothing very interesting in there. The chapel is like a junk room," he explained.

He was partly right. All sorts of objects had been put away there, including a bulletin board detailing the ceremonies for Holy Week—signposting of this kind has proliferated in churches since Vatican II. An old confessional had also been stored there. I had nevertheless observed at the time that the chapel received a lot of visitors, in spite of the bric-a-brac. I had also noticed that no one paid any attention to Heim's decorations. Is it Clesinger's *Pietà* that attracted people?

The chapel is still very much frequented today. One can light a variety of candles there. The *Pietà* is framed by two angels; on her lap the Virgin holds the body of her son taken down from the Cross. The angel on the left laments with mannered stoicism, holding the crown of thorns in his hand like a hoop. This is not so far from Sulpician style, which probably explains its success. People feel at home in the dark retreat of broken hearts and shattered lives.

Its name explains its popularity: the Purgatory Chapel. A place of waiting and suffering before attaining eternal happiness. It is the third realm, an in-between existence that allows for hope. Invented in the twelfth century, purgatory is a dogma hardly ever invoked by Catholic theology today. The belief in a punishment that still has to be undergone before one is admitted to the joy of heaven no doubt suits these men and women in distress. Many are from the French West Indies or originally from Africa. They feel that their suffering is only a transitory state, even here on earth, and that after their time in purgatory, they will see the end of their misfortune. They don't look at Heim's paintings, as they can hardly be seen. Léopold felt the same lack of interest, but for other reasons.

When I questioned my friend about this artist, he mumbled a few vague comments,

"I think he painted a picture of Charles X receiving some painters, or something like that. Of no interest at all: a pure product of academic art...."

"No more academic than your Abel de Pujol," I pointed out to him.

"Abel de Pujol is certainly not as good a painter, but at least he had some daring. Heim is cold. He copies the ancients, but there's no originality, no questioning...."

"How can you say that! The whole chapel is in darkness. The *Pietà* blocks out all the light."

"You're right. They haven't treated François-Joseph very kindly," he said, gazing at his hands with their carefully polished nails. (He likes to call the painters by their first names, not to be offhand, but rather out of a kind of affectionate familiarity.)

I was intrigued by the contrast between the glorious Chapel of the Holy Angels and this gloomy den, visited almost as often as Delacroix's blaze of light. I had noticed that the regular visitors to the Souls in Purgatory made a detour to avoid the Holy Angels, as if the light from this chapel hurt their eyes.

Who was this Heim I had never heard of before?

CHAPTER 7

The Château de Crozes

"I can shirk no longer now, and am the victim of duty," Delacroix writes to George Sand on 19 July 1855.

He expresses these good intentions after another stay at Augerville. He adores his cousin Berryer's château and the musical gatherings, but he feels guilty about neglecting Saint-Sulpice. He has not set foot in the place for seven months. This time he seems determined to get down to work, but after a fortnight he says that he is suffering terribly from the heat: "I've had everything scraped, and you might say I'm laying plaster on with a trowel to patch not only the hollows, but also the parts of the figures that have to be bright, like the flesh and the drapery."

He continues fighting with the wall of the chapel, without having solved the problem of the preparation needed to take painting in oil. It is clear that he has not begun *Wrestling with the Angel*, even though he has a very precise idea of the composition and placement of the characters. He adds: "The pictures will benefit from it, but I nearly developed painters' colic."

The threat of lead poisoning, brought on by breathing the lead in paint, seems to have exhausted him. The walls contain a high proportion of white-lead, a white color that is a real poison. "This is not a good time for me at the moment. I have come back to the church after an interruption of nearly a week. I am working under difficult circumstances. There is no relief from this dreadful heat," he admits on 27 August. Three days later he is feeling better. This improvement is due to the music he hears while working. "There was an extraordinary service at eight o'clock. This music puts me in a rapturous state of mind very favorable to painting."

This elation, however, does not last long, for in reality there is no progress. Writing to Constant Dutilleux, the person to whom he had announced the subject for the Chapel of the Holy Angels five years earlier, he gives him to understand that everything has to be done again because of the coating on the wall. "It was so defective that I have had to more or less prepare the walls again myself by redoing the rough sketch!"

When he feels he is making no headway, Delacroix often makes the only possible decision: escape. On 10 September he takes the train. Destination: the Lot. He will spend a few day at the Château de Crozes, between Brive and Souillac, the home of his sister Henriette de Verninac.

Contact with nature energizes him. He draws and is often alone. Crozes is somewhat neglected. There is grass growing everywhere, but he likes it there. He has already stayed at the château several times. He leaves again after three days. When one considers the length and fatigue of the journey, the shortness of his stay is surprising. All the more so because he has scarcely returned to Paris before he runs off to his Lamey cousins in Strasbourg.

I wanted to see Crozes, although not for any particular reason. Delacroix came to this château in upper Quercy at a difficult time for *Wrestling with the Angel*. I'm weak enough to believe that, hidden behind the apparent immobility of a place there can sometimes be signs—short, quick oscillations that alert the mind. Someone came here. All trace of him has disappeared.

And yet some mark, even if it is infinitesimal, always remains. A whole face can eventually be reconstituted from a spot; a personality can be perceived in a smell. Houses are stained not only with fingerprints, but also with invisible inscriptions that reveal their occupants, even the earliest.

I often think of young Michelet's visit to the Musée des Monuments Français, when he wandered among the headless statues bathed in blue light from the stained-glass windows. The great historian had the gift of going back into time by taking the no-entry lane. He wrote this magnificent statement: "These dead in their tombs who made all times contemporary: I created their history; I caught a glimpse of religion."

Crozes, one August afternoon. I had not notified anyone I was coming. Arriving unexpectedly is an approach that often produces excellent results. Who lives in the château today? A young woman is lying on a chaise lounge in the middle of the lawn, looking slightly disgruntled. I have woken her up. She looks surprised, then anxious. "Delacroix? I'll go in and ask." She elegantly picks up a wide-brimmed straw hat by the crown, places it on her head and holds it there. The hat has a blue braid ending in a tassel. Last century this type of ribbon was called a follow-me-young-man. And what would he ask for?

I imagine that she knows about the painter's connection with Crozes. Perhaps the sudden appearance of a stranger has worried her. I've frightened her and she needs to share her apprehension with someone. An older woman, who turns out to be her mother, appears on the threshold and asks me to come in. She has a quiet, courteous self-assurance and a gracious air about her. Those good manners that one hardly finds anywhere but in the provinces these days immediately make any awkwardness vanish.

Near the piano in the cool, dim drawing room, I can see Delacroix's sister, Henriette de Verninac. The portrait painted by David in 1799 belonged to Delacroix for a short time then passed into the hands of the great collector Charles de Bestegui, who gave it to the Louvre Museum in 1942.

"As you can see, it's only a copy. My family had the original. My grandmother would only agree to part with it if she could have a copy and keep the original frame. In that way we can almost believe that we still have the real portrait, can't we?"

She gave a sad smile. Seventy years later, the sale of that painting is still a wrench for this poor lady who has always worshipped Delacroix. Her grandmother was a Verninac. When the painter died, his cousin François de Verninac inherited many articles, among them David's painting. Delacroix is critical of it in his *Journal*. He had a notion one day to put it beside a Géricault. He can hardly find words severe enough to criticize David's "coldness" and his servile imitation of nature. "All his daring consists of including a fragment, a foot or an arm, moulded from some antique statue, and making his living model as similar as possible to the perfect beauty he saw in the plaster."

What a surprise to find Delacroix's own sister unexpectedly here, in the suffocating heat of summer! She sits familiarly in the drawing room beside the piano, rather than presiding over it. Her presence is reassuring—a domestic god protecting the household, a guardian spirit of her brother Eugène, ironically invoked by David.

"It occasionally strikes me that Henriette has a slightly bovine look, don't you think? I shouldn't say that. Perhaps it's spite," she says with a laugh.

She is not wrong. Henriette in the painting has round cheeks and a glum look that emphasizes the severity of David's drawing technique and his predilection for dryness. Was she a good sister to Delacroix? She took Eugène in after their mother's death in 1814, but he had to pay board. He had to tighten his belt for a long time because of his sister's miserliness. All Delacroix's mother left her children was the property Le Domaine d'Axe, near Mansle in the Charente. It was sold at a loss in 1822. Questions of inheritance caused a coolness between the painter and his sister.

After she was widowed, Henriette had no money and had to find work as a lady's companion to survive. She died in 1827. She had one son, Charles, who inherited the David painting. This spendthrift nephew whom Delacroix adored was reduced to parting with his mother's portrait. It happened twice. Delacroix managed to buy back the painting and hung it in his drawing room.

Another picture next to Henriette intrigues me.

"That one's an original. It's Charles Delacroix, minister of Foreign Affairs under the Directoire and the painter's father. You are no doubt going to say that there is no likeness between father and son."

"That often happens and doesn't prove anything," I reply cautiously.

The "secret" about his birth: one cannot dodge it when the subject of Delacroix comes up. Was Charles the painter's real father? We know that this assertion, which is still debated, claims that Talleyrand was his father. It was originally made by Mme. Jaubert, a habitué of the evening gatherings at Augerville. Mme. Jaubert was an acquaintance of Delacroix and is often mentioned in his *Journal*. In her memoirs, published in 1881, she writes: "Is it necessary to repeat what was sometimes told in whispers, that the yellowish pallor and the very characteristic wry smile could make one think of Prince Talleyrand?" I don't share the opinion of those who think that this matter is purely anecdotal. "The question is of little importance," states Alain Daguerre des Hureaux, one of the most recent commentators on the artist. I am of the opposite opinion: it is a point that should be taken into consideration. It undoubtedly has a connection with *Jacob Wrestling with the Angel.*

Charles Delacroix was born at Givry-en-Argonne (Marne), the son of a bailiff. He began his career as a teacher in a college at Rodez. He came to the notice of Turgot, who at that time was administrator of Limousin province, and became his secretary. When Turgot was appointed controller of Finance in 1774, he took Charles Delacroix to Paris, making him one of his closest collaborators. The disgrace of the man who could have saved the monarchy meant, however, that Delacroix had to give up his post. He welcomed the Revolution, became the representative of the Marne at the convention, and was one of the 397 deputies who voted for the death of the king—there were 334 against.

Before that he was involved in an equally momentous decision: the solemn act of abolishing the monarchy in France, made on 20 September 1792. As secretary of the National Convention, he is one of the three signatories on the document with Vergniaud and Sieyès. When a member of the Council of Elders—the legislative assembly set up by the Thermidorian Convention— he was appointed minister of Foreign Affairs under the Directoire (1795), a post he held until July 1797.

Eugène Delacroix's mother, Victoire Oeben, came from a great family of cabinetmakers. Her father, Jean-François, made the famous Louis XV bureau, although he never finished it. His pupil, Jean-Henri Riesener completed it, and later married his master's widow.

There were various marriages, which often produced many children. This explains the host of cousins and tends to give the impression of a complicated family situation. It also explains the constant trips made by the painter, who loved visiting his numerous relatives.

Eugène Delacroix was born on 26 April 1798 at Charenton-Saint-Maurice. The date of his conception (the end of July or beginning of August in the previous year) corresponds to a time when his father was suffering from a testicular tumor, which ostensibly prevented him from procreating. The excrescence was enormous. "Delacroix is not a minister: he is a pregnant old woman," exclaimed Mme. de Staël. On 13 September 1797, seven months before Eugène's birth, Charles Delacroix decided he would undergo surgery. He stoically put up with an operation without anaesthetic lasting two and a half hours. The tumor weighed thirty pounds, and its removal was the subject of a detailed account with many illustrations published by the surgeon, Ange Imbert-Delonnes.

The case looks simple: Eugène was conceived either at the normal time between the end of July and the beginning of August, or after the operation during the last fortnight in September. In the first instance, Charles Delacroix cannot a priori be the father; in the second, the operation is too close for him to father a child. In theory, there is little likelihood that Charles Delacroix could be the father. In theory. But there can be exceptions to the rule in this area. Anatomical details noted by specialists[1] prove that Charles Delacroix had not lost his virility before the removal of the tumor, and that after that operation, this particularly robust man could recover rapidly and procreate. In that case, Delacroix would have been born prematurely.

"My grandmother Verninac told us time and time again that this story about Talleyrand was ridiculous. Besides, you know that three letters from Charles Delacroix to his wife have been found in the family archives, in this very place, by Paul Loppin, a former judge of the Supreme Court of Appeal. They were written in 1798 when Charles Delacroix was on a mission in Holland. This correspondence leaves no doubt about the trusting, even frank relationship the couple shared."

"That doesn't really prove anything! You must admit that in such circumstances a wife who has been unfaithful to her husband may be particularly affectionate to make up for it. And cuckolded husbands have been known to speak openly."

She does not respond, but does not seem convinced either. We move on to the resemblance between Talleyrand and Eugène Delacroix. The painter's proud tilt of the head has been compared to that of the great man. There is some similarity also in their posture. The same bearing, the same insolent look, the same disdainful mouth, the same high cheekbones. But going from that to finding common characteristics and a blood relationship is more chancy. Talleyrand was fair with a pale complexion; Delacroix had jet black hair and olive skin. If we are to believe Théophile Gautier, he looked like a "Maharaja." Baudelaire mentions "his Peruvian complexion." Nevertheless, wanting to accumulate too much evidence in a way makes the argument suspect.

Did Eugène Delacroix know anything about this question of paternity? André Joubin, who edited Delacroix's *Journal*, states in a footnote that he has in his possession a very rare copy of the famous description of the operation by the surgeon Ange Imbert-Delonnes (another angel![2]). He says that it originally belonged to the painter himself. This information would suggest that Delacroix *knew*. "As he often put his date of birth back a year, one wonders whether he may not have been acting on a desire to make his birth look more regular," comments René

Huyghe, the author of *Delacroix ou le Combat solitaire*, an authoritative work on the painter. "Surely the most important consideration is, finally, the consequences that this doubtful paternity could have had on Delacroix's works?" Barthélemy Jobert, another specialist, quite rightly asks. But he goes on to say, "Wherever one looks, however, there is nothing that can settle the problem one way or the other."

Can one be as categorical as that? Admittedly there is no trace of this controversial question of paternity in the painter's writings (the *Journal* or *Correspondence*). The rumor that he was the son of the apostate bishop went round the salons during his lifetime. The only written mention comes from an art critic, Théophile Silvestre, whom Delacroix knew. He makes the allusion that the painter was "rocked on Talleyrand's knee."

The insinuation probably did not escape those who knew the gossip. Silvestre's pseudorevelation—it has been established that Talleyrand never saw Delacroix—was made in 1856. Delacroix refers to his father with the greatest respect, and mentions the name of Talleyrand only twice in his *Journal*, without ever lingering over it. Nonetheless, the fact that the subject does not appear in his writing does not mean that this sensitive issue was absent from his painting. Who can know the hidden motives that drive the creator, the confusion and complexity of his personal and family affairs, all those latent forces that he has silently metabolized, then brought forth in his work?

The father figure is present in several of his paintings: *The Two Foscari*, for example, in which the doge of Venice must hear the sentence read out condemning his son; or the numerous depictions of Hamlet (Hamlet has the players re-enact the scene where his father is poisoned, Hamlet following his father's ghost, etc.). He even painted himself as the prince of Denmark. The story of this Shakespearean hero obviously obsessed the artist. "No one has felt the tragic character of Hamlet as deeply as Delacroix," his friend George Sand remarked.

As for Jacob attacked by an angel as he is about to cross the Jabbok ford, whom should he fear? His brother Esau, whose birthright he has stolen? No doubt. But even more his father Isaac, whom he has tricked. Did he not steal from him the blessing meant for his brother? Contrary to Barthélemy Jobert's opinion, I think that these questions have resonated in the creation of *Wrestling with the Angel*.

Nearly all families have a skeleton in the cupboard. Why should the Delacroixs be any different? The family story is not kind to Eugène: uncertain paternity, an ungenerous sister, a brother killed at the Battle of Friedland who was never mentioned, Charles-Henry, the eldest, who, unlike his brother, was talked about too much and who was supposed to be the original of that scoundrel Philippe Bridau in Balzac's *La Rabouilleuse*. One thing is certain: at the time when Jacob is about to undergo the supreme test, a heavy liability exists between himself, his father Isaac, and his brother Esau.

But let us return to Crozes, this summer afternoon, and to my hostess. She gives me a rather humorous account of visits by Delacroix specialists poaching the family archives, but carefully hiding the aim of their pursuit. Crozes still contains treasures. Many papers have not yet been examined. She shows me the painter's seven or eight embroidered waistcoats and his Academician's sword. He wanted that sword so badly. He finally received it on 10 January 1857, at the time when he was working hardest at Saint-Sulpice. He had applied six times.

A few days before the election, he had made the visits traditionally required of the candidate. Whom did he meet on 3 January? None other than François-Joseph Heim, his "neighbor" at Saint-Sulpice. The decoration of the Chapel of the Souls in Purgatory had been finished long before Delacroix began his task on the other side of the wall. He never mentions the fact that their work is in adjoining chapels. The only allusion to Heim is in the *Journal*, concerning a visit to Strasbourg, which took place five days after his trip to Crozes—a strange coincidence. In the municipal museum he lingers in front of a painting by Heim entitled *Shepherd Drinking at a Fountain* to look closely at a nude figure that catches his eye. "This man had a feeling something like that of the Italian masters," he notes. He adds—and this is the most important point— "This picture is in a very bad state; I see his last great picture there, exhibited two years ago and since then rolled up and left in a corner, just as it was delivered. That is how provincial museums treat paintings" (19 September 1855).

Heim is already on the way to being forgotten. Delacroix speaks of him in the past tense, as if he were dead, although the two men will be brought together later. What does Delacroix think of his colleague? The reference to the Italian masters naturally implies a compliment from the admirer of Raphael and Veronese, but his sympathy for Heim's misfortune seems to apply to the whole profession and above all to himself.

Heim, the painter now excluded and cast aside. One cannot help but be surprised at his fate, and yet it is not the first time an artist, above all a defender of the academic tradition, has experienced it. But should he be described as purely academic? His path often crossed Delacroix's. When Delacroix was painting the library in the Palais Bourbon at the beginning of the 1840s, Heim was decorating the Salle des Conférences. There was a third painter, none other than Abel de Pujol, who was working on the ceiling in the Salle des Distributions.

Delacroix, Heim, Abel de Pujol: they are together well before Saint-Sulpice. "What will remain of Messrs. Heim and Abel de Pujol? Who will remember their names in ten years' time?" Gustave Planche, the critic for the *Revue des Deux Mondes* asks in 1851. He then replies, rather unkindly, to his own question: "They teach drawing, they know the lines and contours sanctioned by tradition; yet they have not conceived or produced anything that merits discussion, and for twenty-nine years, M. Delacroix has the advantage of attracting attention with the originality and the variety of his works." A final judgment, if ever there was one! Yet Gustave Planche was a great admirer of the classics and, given everything about him, he should have been inclined to appreciate Heim.

At Crozes, I keep coming back to look at the Academician's sword with the superfine ridge on its blade. Did Delacroix often grasp that pommel? I'm fascinated by the hand guard.

Certain dwellings seem to encapsulate moments in our history in unexpected ways. Crozes is one of them. Apart from memories of Delacroix, it also contains relics that belonged to ministers of the Third Republic, a colonial governor, etc. These ghosts live here on good terms under the benevolent leadership of my hostess, although she would never think of boasting about it.

Delacroix's Academician's uniform is a little faded. The jacket looks very narrow. It is true that in the photographs of him that still exist, he has a thin torso and narrow shoulders. The slight, almost fragile build contrasts strongly with his imperious bearing. "This intense, expressive, mobile face sparkled with wit, genius, and passion," Théophile Gautier remarked.

There is no photograph of him in his institute costume. Taking his role seriously, he assiduously attended meetings, even if he was sometimes seen to put on superior airs with his colleagues. Thus he notes in his *Journal* after the general meeting of the institute: "The sight of all these faces amused me." Belated revenge compensating for the humiliating refusals and relative disaffection he believed were directed at him at that time. He cannot bear the idea of being taken for the representative of a past era, that of the romantic school. The painter of *Liberty Leading the People* does not see himself as a revolutionary. This reputation frustrates the admirer of the classics in him. Delacroix often expressed his strong dislike of dreamers, sentimentality, and "lachrymose style."

Two years before his election to the institute, the year 1855 gives him a brilliant opportunity to compensate for all his wrongs. The World Exhibition shows thirty-six of his paintings including *The Massacre at Chios, The Women of Algiers in their Quarters, The Taking of Constantinople by the Crusaders.* Two months later his reputation is established. He is promoted to commander of the Legion of Honor and receives one of the exhibition's grand medals. Another painter, who had definitely been forgotten, is also restored to favor. Like Delacroix he receives the grand medal and is made an officer of the Legion of Honor. His name: François-Joseph Heim, still nearby Delacroix or following in his wake! So incompatible, yet so close. As Delacroix was convinced that the path to glory was through the institute, he must therefore have known Heim's most famous painting: *Charles X Rewarding Artists at the Close of the 1824 Exhibition.* That is the year of *The Massacre at Chios* (and also the year when Delacroix stopped keeping his *Journal*, which he does not take up again until 1847).

Heim and Delacroix are honored at the same time. I wonder if they spoke to each other on that occasion?

Today Heim's painting hangs in a room in the Louvre, which, as fate would have it, bears Delacroix's name. It is relegated to a spot high up on the wall, and one cannot see the expressions on the host of faces that the painter took such pains to depict.

It is obvious that proximity to Delacroix brought him no luck at all.

As the afternoon draws to a close at Crozes, the shadows fall and the air is cooler. The château comes to life. We go out into the garden to have refreshments near the hundred-year-old box bushes cut into the shape of spheres. At the close of day, they give off an ancient, acrid smell.

"These bushes were here in Delacroix's time," the hostess tells me. "We take extremely good care of them."

We suddenly realize that we are all taking deep breaths of evening air. As well as the pungent smell from the box bushes, there is the faint spicy odor of old books, rather like cloves.

I seem to detect the faded smell of the Academician's costume I was examining earlier. The smell of Delacroix.

CHAPTER 8

Delacroix's Cigars

On 23 February 1856, Delacroix complains of "an unbearable smell" in the chapel. He sends off his assistant Andrieu to inquire about it. Since the trip to Crozes, work has been put off or held in abeyance, as his artistic commitments elsewhere are extremely demanding. It seems that the bad smell is coming from an accumulation of rubbish under the floor.

From 1854 to 1861 the chapel is cluttered with a system of guy ropes and racks. It is an entrenched camp bristling with scaffolding and ladders. A good deal of the equipment is hired from the firm of Auguste Bellu. From his platform, Delacroix lays siege to the wall, but cannot come to grips with it. It is slow and often discouraging, undermining labor.

On 17 March 1856, the *Journal* states once again: "Andrieu has begun work at the church." Delacroix seems determined to get back to his task. He calls on one of his pupils, Louis Boulangé, to see to the background and speed up the work. He calls a meeting at Saint-Sulpice on 20 March. Delacroix wants to make an objective judgment of how much has been accomplished after an interruption of five months. He is disappointed. "I stubbornly went on for too long last year. I spent too much effort working from false premises." The only thing making progress is the painting of the Archangel Michael. On 6 May, he declares: "We are drawing the cartoon sketch for the ceiling."

*   *   *

Jacob Wrestling with the Angel and *Heliodorus* sometimes make one forget the ceiling of the chapel showing the *Archangel Michael Slaying the Demon*. Although this work gave him fewer technical concerns—it is a canvas mounted on the wall—it always suffers by comparison with the two mural paintings. Many critics have slated it. Among Delacroix's contemporaries, Baudelaire devotes only one paragraph to it in his account of the artist's work. He talks of "a highly dramatic magnificence," which is fairly noncommittal. On the other hand, he notices that "the strong light, coming through the window occupying the upper part of the exterior wall, obliges the viewer to make a considerable effort to enjoy the painting properly." Too true. One has to look up very high, at the risk of dislocating one's neck, to catch the details. Lucifer piteously gripping his pitchfork may raise a smile, but the downfall of the Prince of Darkness is illuminated by the strangeness of the aquamarine landscape.

Another halt halfway through June. At the beginning of July, Delacroix retreats once again to his little house at Champrosay. He takes the air in the Sénart forest and lingers at two trees he often mentions in his *Journal*. The Prieur oak and the Antin oak have played a major part in his inspiration. For a long time now he has gone on these walks especially to see the two trees with their enormous trunks. The Antin oak amazes him, and he finds it "frighteningly huge." "I sat down facing this giant," he notes on 5 July. He is also fascinated by the oak next to it.

"No woman would have been visited more often than the Prieur oak in its forest glory, and none would have been drawn so often," Yves Florenne points out perceptively.[1] The tree is linked to genealogy and is at the origin of the Fall. In the Garden of

Eden from which man has been cast out for ever, the Tree of Life is henceforth guarded by angels.

The shade from three huge trees dominates the scene of the struggle in *Jacob Wrestling with the Angel*. A few rays of light pierce the depths of the forest like glimmers of a fire from afar. Delacroix admired the way Corot painted trees. It was at Champrosay that he came to understand their "principles." He specifies that they should be "built up in tints of light like flesh." He learns that lesson brilliantly in Saint-Sulpice.

For a long time the monumental spread of branches in these trees, covering the struggle with their silent strength, rather minimized the importance of Jacob and the angel for me. I could see their fight only as a silly, muddle-headed brawl. The real thrust of the fight is there, in those three trees: a telluric pressure coming from the bowels of the earth, surging out triumphantly throughout the vast waving branches of the three giants.

Champrosay is Delacroix's *querencia*, a place that offers protection, withdrawal, and temporary disengagement while he reflects on his counterattack. When he takes refuge there, you may be sure that work at Saint-Sulpice is progressing. He loves picking dandelions with Jenny and watching trails of ants in the forest. The wild painter of tigers tearing at horses is more and more fascinated by the lives of tiny creatures. He spends hours watching "a slug with exactly the same spots as a panther: wide rings on its back" (*Journal*, 15 October 1856).

Delacroix, who is fifty-eight at the time, has only seven more years to live. In that year of 1856, Delacroix has begun to make his will, meticulously drawing up a list of his inheritors. He is suffering from tubercular laryngitis, the illness that will finally kill him. A varicocele[2] that had affected him at the end of the

1840s torments him once again. This testicular complaint flares up just when he is working hardest on Jacob. The nature of his work means that he is always either standing or perched up on a ladder, increasing his discomfort.

This extremely reserved man, exquisitely and coldly urbane—Baudelaire remarks that he had "twenty ways of saying *Mon cher Monsieur*"—discourages any kind of familiarity. He has to control an excitable, passionate temperament (but at what cost!). This contradiction did not escape some of his more astute contemporaries. "He was velvety smooth and caressing, like one of those tigers whose amazingly subtle grace he caught so magnificently," Théophile Gautier writes in a famous pen portrait. "A marvelously easy manner…the tiger paying attention to its prey," says Baudelaire, who knew what he was talking about. "Handsome as a tiger, with the same pride, the same finesse, the same strength," remarks Odilon Redon, going one better, on seeing him in 1859.

The tiger, the leopard, the feline. The same comparison with these carnivorous animals is taken up later by Gauguin to describe his technique ("Delacroix's drawing always reminds me of the strong, supple movements of a tiger"). One would think they had passed the word around, and in the end the image becomes a stereotype. Actually, the first to speak of Delacroix's "feline grace" is the journalist Théophile Silvestre in 1855.

There is a stealthy cruelty running through the *Journal*. Reading its pages, one can feel the thrill of Delacroix hunting in silence, noiselessly strangling his contemporaries, then coming back alone to his lair at Champrosay. This fierce, sadistic side of Delacroix, that Baudelaire liked so much, also appeals to our age. And yet the way the poet, lost in admiration, was ever so courteously dropped by the master after an initially cordial reception, must have left a bad memory. Baudelaire's name appears only four times in the *Journal*, to which should be added the mention of four visits by "Dufaÿs," the pseudonym Baudelaire used at one time. This disguise, uncovered by Armand Moss,[3] is strangely enough not picked up in the *Journal* annotated by André Joubin.

Using this name of Dufaÿs, which came from his mother, Baudelaire shamelessly went so far as to ask the painter to lend him money in 1847. This surprising fact is never referred to whenever the subject of the relationship between the two men comes up. Delacroix himself mentions the name of Baudelaire two years later, without any allusion to the Dufaÿs he had helped earlier. The extraordinary links between the two men are legendary. At that time one was at the height of his fame, while the other seemed a failure. If Delacroix appreciated Baudelaire's praise, he paid no attention to his poetry and had no understanding of this odd character, so foreign to his own temperament and milieu. "There is a kind of incomprehensible disjointedness in his ideas, which does not suit my turn of mind," he notes quite scornfully on 30 May 1856. The dandy poet was an impossible person, but he went to great lengths to please Delacroix. He just wanted to be liked and the master would not give him that. Before he died, however, Baudelaire revealed his bitterness, referring to the painter as "a great egotist."[4] Fantin-Latour's famous painting, *Homage to Delacroix*, features Baudelaire, Manet, Braquemond, Legros, and Whistler. None of them was a follower of the master—except one, Baudelaire. As Philippe Jullian maintains, he is Delacroix's only disciple.

It is impossible to fit Delacroix neatly into any category. He never belonged to the bohemian world of Paris; he hated their habits and their eccentricity. Although born into an upper-middle-class family, he had to earn his living very early in his life.

His childhood was poor and the fear of being without always haunted him. "I understood early on how indispensable it is for a man in my position to have a certain amount of money. [...] Dignity and respect for him as a person come only with being able to live in reasonable comfort."

He managed his money prudently, chose his investments, bought shares in the Burgundy Canal. He also kept meticulous accounts of his expenditures—the obsessive calculations in his notebooks on show at the Delacroix Museum in the rue Fursten- berg are incredible. During the time he is working at Saint- Sulpice, his paintings are selling well, he is well off, but he has always had a modest lifestyle: "I like moderation; I detest any- thing sumptuous or showy." Although he criticizes the social round, he can still conform to it in great style. In his memoirs, the writer Arsène Houssaye describes him as "the liveliest, most unpredictable, most brilliant host one could have." He adds: "He kept an exquisite table."

This is not an aspect that is often mentioned. One sees only the artist burning with enthusiasm for his work. The high demands, the intellectual fervor, the concern for beauty found throughout the *Journal* should not make us forget Delacroix the great lover of good food. At the beginning of the year, he scrupulously keeps a note of the Bordeaux he has ordered, is interested in the qual- ity of the various vintages, and shows a real curiosity about enol- ogy. He knows for example that if the old vines give a low yield, their quality is excellent.

The year 1856 in the *Journal* thus begins with reminders about addresses for English and Mayence hams. On 10 April he notes: "Payment to Bouchereau, 575 francs." Bouchereau is his Bordeaux wine merchant.

Delacroix tells a story that says a lot about the importance he accorded to gastronomy. He is talking about the death of one Dugas, a restaurateur renowned for his excellent pâtés. Not only did he die without revealing the secret of his recipe, but he also disinherited his sons. "This is the character trait of the artist," Delacroix comments, not without irony, but still with some admiration.

A bad cigar can make him ruin a picture. I have an order form in Delacroix's name from La Civette du Palais-Royal. It would seem he was a good customer and eclectic in his tastes, as he liked both Havana and Manila cigars. Judging by his account books, he was smoking a lot of them when he was working on the Chapel of the Holy Angels. Delacroix seems to fit the definition of the hedonistic puritan: he makes a sober, almost austere use of pleasure. "It is necessary to limit oneself," "to be content," "a superior person knows when to stop" he writes many times over. One must always come back to the *Journal*. It teaches us as much about Delacroix's physical existence as it does about his heart and mind.

This text is a subtle odyssey of the five senses. The sharpest is obviously sight, although with him the visual faculty remains linked to touch and smell. A perfume stirs him deeply, suddenly and unexpectedly bringing back his youth. "I can convince myself that I am happy just from the memory of my past happiness." When Delacroix mentions flesh tints and his ambition to depict "the transparency of blood on skin," the painter is speaking as someone who is aware of the texture and density of human flesh. He knows that touch and sight are equally involved. The eye can feel things. At the very beginning, *Wrestling with the Angel* is a matter of making contact. Delacroix anxiously runs his hand over the wall he is to cover. He feels its hollows, mounds, and valleys. How can he smooth this surface and get rid of the unevenness?

Even today one can plainly see the pressure on the wall, with its asymmetrical sweeps, its smoother surfaces and others that are less even. The crossing or juxtaposition of the brushstrokes sometimes looks like the work of a weaver. Could these raised stitches conceal a hidden motif? Henry James called it "the figure in the carpet." Perhaps its presence cannot be seen, as in Poe's *Stolen Letter*. Against the light, the impasto of oil, resin and wax, and the hatching give the impression of a surface that has been hammered by the brush. The Historic Monuments' research laboratory has identified an incredible number of layers—the angel's robe has up to thirteen.[5]

Wrestling with the Angel is a painting with an uneven, hilly surface—the artist admired the thickness of Rubens' paint and the way it stood out from the canvas. It sometimes looks like roughcast. Delacroix became disheartened. "Matter always falls back into sadness," he wrote one day. (That could be Baudelaire!) He kneaded the empty wall, produced mountainous folds that he then proceeded to even out. Nevertheless, *Wrestling with the Angel* is still uneven and slightly corrugated. There was something of the sculptor in Delacroix.

Sometimes he could stand being shut up in his chapel-cell no longer. Like all prisoners, he would helplessly strike the wall. Behind it he thought he would find deliverance.

CHAPTER 9

An Angel Between the Towers

First October 1998, 9:30 A.M. I am on my way as usual to devote myself to Delacroix. Coming out of the Luxembourg on to the rue Bonaparte, I can make out an unusual crowd of people in the distance on the Place Saint-Sulpice. People are standing near the town hall of the Sixth *arrondissement*, all staring in the direction of the church. Their faces are tense. The policemen look tough and focussed, indicating that something serious is happening. I quicken my pace.

A tightrope walker is suspended in space between the two towers. He is almost halfway across. There is a strong wind and the rope dancer is obviously having trouble keeping his balance. He floats, sways, trying to stay still. Sometimes the balancing pole he is holding wobbles dangerously. It looks as if he is beating his wings. The spread of the counterbalance and the fragility of the tightrope walker make one think of a dragonfly's body, with the abdomen in the shape of a stick.

"It's an angel!" exclaims a light voice from the crowd.

"If the angel swoops, it won't be long before he's back in heaven!" a male voice replies.

His bad joke brings a disapproving murmur from the crowd. They whisper their admiration for the courage and the devil-may-care attitude of the man balancing so high above their heads.

"The wire isn't tight enough. He's going to fall!"

"The wind . . . It's the wind that's giving him trouble."

"Not at all. He knows what he's doing. Look, he's waiting for a lull."

"He looks cold."

Everyone has something to say about it. Gusts of wind blow the jets of water in the fountain backward, splashing the square and sending out a mist of fine droplets. The customers of the Café de la Mairie come out to see the balancing act and those on the terrace are already standing. A hearse pulling up in front of the church adds to the general confusion. The undertakers, usually more composed, are not sure what expression they should adopt. Their eyes are fixed on the tightrope walker in danger as they absentmindedly take out the funeral wreaths. The faces in the crowd express the same indecision as the man standing still on his wire. The family of the departed has just arrived.

"That's all we needed!" exclaims a waiter from the café. "Things could take a turn for the worse if the bell starts tolling"

"Can't you see! The north tower...That's where the bells are. They make a hell of a noise! The surprise will make him lose his footing."

A group of men suddenly appear on the roof of the church. They walk carefully across the balcony. "The firemen!" someone murmurs. I find myself thinking that the church has rarely been looked at with such anxiety. It is early autumn, and the two towers painted by Delacroix in 1824 stand out very clearly in the morning air. The forest of columns extending across the facade emphasize more than ever the theatricality of the church and the drama of these aerial acrobatics. All that can be heard now is the murmur of the fountain.

One has to peer really hard to see the line made by the rope suspended between the towers. It seems dangerously slack. The step the acrobat is attempting makes the cable even looser, but, at the same time, he uses this lack of tension like a spring. He gives several bounds and almost reaches the south tower, but a series of gusts make him lose his balance. The rod dips. The acrobat has trouble controlling his body. He goes down on his right knee. "Oh!" the onlookers gasp. With this genuflection, the hero seems to be begging for mercy. But to whom? To the wind? And the gusts of wind actually die down.

A moment later, he reaches the south tower, using the rope like a springboard. A real vanishing trick taking us from imminent fall to final triumph. The tightrope walker raises his arms in the air as a sign of victory. Several of the spectators shrug their shoulders, as if regretting their fear. The crowd has already forgotten all about it. The funeral service can begin. Everything returns to normal.

The two sides of the great entrance door slowly part, which they do only for funerals and the Sunday high mass. There is something majestic in the way they open. This, no doubt, is because of the seven entrance bays separating the huge mass of the fluted columns. The two immense panels slide and fold back with a grating sound. The sight has a barbaric beauty, emphasized by the inscription that can still be made out on the tympanum over the door: *The French people recognize the Supreme Being and the immortality of the soul.* The lettering is indented, shaded Didot, much used during the Revolutionary period. Efforts have obviously been made to rub it out, but it can still be seen. It is a relic of the time when the "the Temple of Saint-Sulpice," disaffected following the decree of the thirteenth Brumaire year II, was dedicated to the Goddess Reason.

Whenever the monumental, grey-veined oak door opens, the

look of Saint-Sulpice changes. The wide gap suddenly lightens the weight of the heavy facade. The church begins to breathe. The opening causes a strange phenomenon, first by splitting the nave with a ray of light, which then flows out into the half-light inside the church, like the meeting of two rivers whose waters merge. I have seen the coffin of Louis Malle pass through this door while Miles Davis played *Lift to the Scaffold*. I also remember the silence when Marcello Mastroianni's coffin left the church. As soon as the funeral cortege left, the crowd broke into applause.

Funeral services suit Saint-Sulpice. They light it up and even give it an almost joyful atmosphere. It is not a church that naturally inspires meditation. Huysmans compared it to a railway station. It is too proud, too definite, not reflective enough—light penetrates straight into it—and in that, it is certainly not Sulpician.

Don't imagine, however, that "Sulpician style" is dead. Around the square, fashion boutiques have taken the place of the shops selling devotional objects. The two industries are strangely similar: they have the same inhuman air of bigotry and suffering. Skinny mannequins and emaciated virgins are not so different from each other: they have the same mystique of mortification, the same affliction of the flesh, the same sadness.

The burial mass is short. The great door opens on to the Visconti Fountain, known as the "cardinal points" fountain although none of the four bishops on it ever received the purple robe. From the doorway I can see Fénelon's head enveloped in a light mist. He was ordained in Saint-Sulpice and expounded the Holy Scripture there for three years. Next to him on the fountain, his old enemy Bossuet looks directly at the Yves Saint Laurent boutique, but gives the impression that he is watching his neighbor out of the corner of his eye.

There are not many present for the ceremony. Only a dozen people to remember and sum up a life. That is not very many, especially in Saint-Sulpice, where the church looks empty even when there is a crowd. The departed is obviously not a draw card. Everyone goes about their own interests: the tourists, the faithful, the idlers perform their usual ballet around the chapels and past the bays, while the priest tries to inspire some meditation in the meager congregation at the moment of the absolution.

Now I can make my escape. The heart of the great church is beating regularly again. Outside, the funeral attendants smoke discreetly as they wait for the ceremony to end. They hold their cigarettes in the palm of their hands and go behind the hearse to exhale the smoke. I think I can see the tightrope walker near the police station. There are people standing around him. His hair is disheveled, he has a fine moustache, and a cajoling smile, which he frequently subverts by winking slyly.

"If the priest makes a complaint, you've had it."

The person talking to the tightrope walker is a police inspector. He is very smartly dressed in a shirt with Italian collar and a floral silk tie with an opulent knot. His tone with the acrobat is quite gentle, almost paternal.

"You see, there are too many people breaking the rules. It's the thing today to climb the church at night right up to the top of one of the two towers. It's absolutely forbidden. You've gone too far, if I can put it that way."

"It's the climbers who go too far. I only walk. It's not the same thing."

He speaks with a foreign accent. The inspector, who is not sure whether this remark is impertinent or not, decides not to respond. But he makes himself more explicit.

"It's worse. You let yourself be shut in the church at night."

"I did let myself be shut in, that's true. But I had to pick up my equipment."

"What's more, you had an accomplice!"

The tightrope walker looks embarrassed, and says nothing.

"Once again, it's not up to me. It's the priest's decision. Goodbye, and please don't do it again. You frightened the life out of us."

I go up to the acrobat who mumbles when the inspector moves away, "Of course I'll do it again. He doesn't understand. For a tightrope walker, those two towers are a challenge."

"What's so special about them?"

"You'd think they were built specially for us. One hundred five feet between the two! It's easy to rig up the cable. And at nearly two hundred feet up the view is fantastic. Even for you down in the square! Look! The two towers frame the space like a picture and bring out the play of light and movement in the sky."

He tells me that he had once crossed the Thames on a wire. He adds, not without some pride, that on that occasion he caused a traffic jam lasting for two hours.

"But sadly a tightrope walker is no angel! He doesn't fly," he says with a laugh, "he walks, he moves slowly and laboriously over empty space. It's neither solid nor liquid, but that space is still incredibly full. The void beneath the tightrope walker can drown him more surely than water and bury him more deeply than earth," he declares a little sententiously.

He speaks to me enthusiastically about Saint-Sulpice, "the finest church in Paris." I can see that he is very familiar with its history and architecture. And Delacroix? "I wanted to pay homage to him," he assures me. When I show my surprise at the unusual way he expresses this admiration, he replies, "Come on. Let's go and see him."

As we enter the church, the coffin is going out the portico. The funeral service is over. One of the people following the casket is holding a bottle of mineral water in his hand. The tightrope walker makes his way toward the Chapel of the Holy Angels.

"Up there I was struggling like Jacob," he says as a joke.

"Certainly. But it's a different kind of fight."

"*Wrestling with the Angel* is also a story about balance. Look at them both. They are two forces of equal strength acting in opposite directions. This painting is based on the principle of the composition of forces, in other words, balance."

"But that doesn't mean Jacob and the angel do acrobatics on a wire."

"No, but you must admit that they are in an unstable balance. It's actually the angel who is doing most of the work. Everything depends on him. His right leg is strong and steady. And look at his left arm keeping him balanced like my pole! It compensates admirably for Jacob's thrust. This angel is a model for me. I thought of him all the time I was up there on the wire."

"But you can't reduce this painting to a point about balance.... "

"Of course not! Jacob is facing this test alone. He has moved aside everything surrounding him: family, servants, flocks. He is going to make his way across."

"Well then, you are Jacob! You step across the void; you go from the north to the south tower; it's your Jabbok ford?"

"I've told you. My model is the angel. Jacob is more the adversary, my own void. The angel has to conquer it.... "

I try to draw his attention to the *Heliodorus* painting, to the flying angel whipping the man on the ground. It's useless. He is not interested in it.

I suddenly understand why. Heliodorus is clumsy on his feet. He has lost his balance.

CHAPTER 10

1998

"You have come to listen to music, not to words." An evening concert in May at Saint-Sulpice. One of those brilliant days when the light takes ages to fade. The chirping of the swifts as they skim the fountain can be heard even inside the church.

I am standing behind a lectern beside the high altar, feeling ill at ease. The audience, who have come to hear a concert dedicated to the memory of Eugène Delacroix, are looking at me enquiringly. I can sense the silence, one of those heavy, very attentive silences that come from embarrassment or excessive urbanity. One can never know which. The audience is made up of Saint-Sulpice parishioners and music lovers—not mutually exclusive as well as admirers of the painter. There in the very first row I notice the lecturer from the Louvre and some members of her expensively dressed group. She gives me a little nod of encouragement. It is true that I am not exactly blowing my own trumpet.

The date is 26 May 1998. The concert has been organized by the Association for the Promotion of the Great Organ of Saint-Sulpice and is one of several events to mark the two hundredth anniversary of Delacroix's birth. There are no fewer than nine exhibitions across France commemorating it! The next time something like this happens will be in 2063, the two hundredth anniversary of his death. Soon "the year of Delacroix" will be no more than a memory. The critics have seized the opportunity presented by the bicentennial of his birth to "situate" the painter with regard to our "modernity," and to produce new "expert assessments" of his work.

When I tentatively accepted the invitation, I thought I could probably get out of it later. Once again I had pinned too much faith on some very weak excuses. The day came and I had not been able to cancel. The invitations had been sent and my name was on them with a few of my own words. They also had a quotation from Maurice Sérullaz. I was flattered to be in such company. Maurice Sérullaz, who died in 1997, is recognized as one of the best Delacroix specialists. I had gone to see him a few months before his death—he lived in Paris in the rue...Eugène Delacroix. He was the chief organizer of the great retrospective put together for the centenary of the artist's death in 1963. His book, *Les Peintures murales d'Eugène Delacroix*, is a classic.

During the conversation I had with Maurice Sérullaz, he told me he was convinced that Charles Delacroix was indeed Eugène's father, "even though one can't be sure of anything where such things are concerned," he added. We also talked about the bitumen Delacroix used in his preparations. This technique has blackened some of his pictures. Copal varnish has yellowed others. He loved to try new techniques, but in his last years he had to admit that these modern methods had had a disastrous effect. "All these paintings will soon perish," he prophesied in 1857. "He didn't tar the surface of *Wrestling with the Angel*," Sérullaz explained to me, "but the painting has become much duller because of the draughts. The entrance door almost opens on to the chapel. Imagine how fresh the colors must have been when he finished in 1861. It's still dazzling, but less than it was. That is something we find hard to measure today."

Why mention this in a concert given in memory of Delacroix? Everyone knows me at Saint-Sulpice. The head priest of the parish and his assistants, the sacristan and his aides, the lady who sells postcards in the sacristy, all the permanent workers in the church are aware of my activities. They tolerate my behavior, which must seem strange to them, and show me not only understanding but also, I think, a certain kindness. My obsession must amuse them. Essentially I am a kind of Quasimodo of Saint-Sulpice, a soul who limps around getting in the way, smitten by a bizarre passion for this church-Esmeralda. The sacristan with his invariable politeness regularly inquires, "What have you found in the Chapel of the Holy Angels?" Ever since I told him about a "hidden meaning" in *Wrestling with the Angel*, he keeps informed as to how my research is progressing. I have also been seen on television talking about Delacroix's chapel in a program called *The Day of the Lord*. Among the regulars at Saint-Sulpice, I would be considered one of the eccentrics. There are a few others: the tramp in the rue Palatine—the spitting image of the painter Courbet—the heavy-hearted supplicants in the Chapel of the Souls in Purgatory, the young beggar at the entrance of the church, who holds out his hand so politely.

As we know, the organ inspired Delacroix when he was painting in the Holy Angels. George Sand believed that, "He would probably have been a great musician if he had not chosen to be a great painter." His favorite composers were Mozart, Cimarosa, and Beethoven. He felt a strong friendship toward Chopin, the only contemporary to find favor in his eyes.

Tonight we will hear three Chopin Preludes. The guest organist, Gabriel Marghieri, himself a composer, has written a piece entitled *Jacob Wrestling with the Angel*, which he will play later. Before the concert, he told me about his fascination with the organ at Saint-Sulpice. "It has strength and mystery. The consistency and the smoothness of its timbres are very similar to Delacroix's colors," he confided to me. "All organists are fascinated by the Cavaillé instrument in Saint-Sulpice. It can produce countless halftones, colors that are often deep and dark, and it has a wonderful capacity for allowing the musical discourse to expand and fill space." He used colors when speaking about the organ....

I am introducing each of these pieces, describing Delacroix's relationship with music, and above all commenting on the paintings in the Chapel of the Holy Angels. As they are an integral part of their wall, they scorn retrospective exhibitions. The occasion could seem quite intoxicating for someone so fond of Saint-Sulpice, but I have no illusions about this privilege, conferred on me because of past trials and tribulations. Why try to deny it: some people have also come to observe the ex-hostage in Lebanon.[1] This voyeurism is rarely ill-intentioned, I know. I am resigned to seeing it come into my life imperceptibly like an old acquaintance who has shared a terrible ordeal with me and whom I cannot get rid of.

I cannot separate this unwanted companion who makes my life a misery from my unique, conscious and permanent self. It is my personal disaster area. It needs to be left in darkness and silence to recover from the devastation. Sometimes I tend to forget the damage, which is not all collateral, but the look in other people's eyes is always there to remind me. I cannot do anything about it. I am resigned to having my memory pricked in this way. Besides, our time is interested only in the person's function, not in the person him or herself. I have been locked into a role and labeled, like "the peace-time philosopher," "Mitterand's faithful but critical ex-cabinet minister," or "the bankrupt but happy

start-up whiz-kid." "Former hostage" is the social raison d'être
that has been allotted to me.

Those who have followed my misadventure at all closely will
know that this role includes a special feature: I am the former
hostage who, *in addition*, has rediscovered his faith. I must therefore be a bit of a mystic, or in other words, a visionary. This
evening's talk matches my role perfectly. I am also conscious of
helping to maintain this character who is not me, or is only a
part of me.

He might not have a mass, but Delacroix certainly deserves a
concert. And I have not rediscovered my faith for the simple reason that I never lost it. I have also resigned myself to these sup-
positions people make, which at least provide something to joke
about. These misunderstandings do not embarrass me, let alone
cause me pain. They are part of the great universal joke. There is
a comic element in every tragedy, which is generally concealed
on the pretext that misfortune cannot include a mixture of gen-
res. It is almost taboo to observe that the two are intermingled.
All that concerns us is the opinion of others. Man loves others to
feel sorry for him; he cannot bear anything in the slightest way
ridiculous, which would lessen the impact of his misfortune.

I happen to have a particular liking for the ridiculous heroes of
literature. Don Quixote, among others. There is a kind of artless-
ness and freedom in the ridiculous that I find touching. Jean-
Jacques Rousseau confessing, "I'm ridiculous," moves me more
than Voltaire, that dry soul so often paralyzed by human respect,
and who so frequently uses the word *ridiculous* as a weapon
against his adversaries. Those who have dared to brave mockery
have conquered the world. On the day of the eighteenth Brumaire, deputies from the Council of the Five Hundred[2] made
fun of Bonaparte, who appeared quite ludicrous, but who took no

notice. During His Passion, Christ accepted not only the stick in place of a scepter but also being an object of scorn. There is an element of the tragic in the ridiculous: naïveté reveals the ludicrous side of the human condition. The ridiculous person is one of the pure in heart; he is unaware of what is happening and, like Don Quixote, he fights while people make fun of him behind his back. In the end, the only reproach one can make of Eugène Delacroix, the man, is a fear of ridicule.

Baudelaire has described his "sarcastic mood" and his "supreme cynicism." For Delacroix, a man of the eighteenth century, the main fault of his rival Ingres is "the ridiculous, which predominates to a very high degree." His irony discreetly permeates the pages of his *Journal* as a means of protection. Delacroix playing the derisive lord of the manor is without peer. He feigns ignorance and metes out disapproval under the guise of praise. This attitude contrasts strangely with the way he puts himself in danger when he paints. From *Sardanapalus* to the 1859 salon, he is admired but often ridiculed as well.

It must be said that I have no illusions about the significance of my performance. Besides, why should it be significant? I'm not there to preach a sermon. But, after all, I have taken the priest's place here behind my lectern. There is something comical, even ridiculous—that word again—about this talk. The way one puts one's oar in while not really being justified in doing so, that's me this evening. So many famous voices have rung out under these arches: Bossuet, the Great Condé! I make sure to remind my audience of them. In the deathly hush, I also mention the fact that the Marquis de Sade and Baudelaire were baptized in this church. And Talleyrand... The lecturer from the Louvre shifts in her seat. I can't tell from her expression whether she is delighted or annoyed, she who so often quotes Baudelaire.

Now I come to Delacroix. I point out the fact that this agnostic frequently went into churches. "He may not have had any feeling for religion, but he certainly is a great religious painter," I say with a rather acrobatic turn of phrase. Of course Delacroix's contradictory, even paradoxical attitude to religion should be explained. He was a man of the Enlightenment—although also convinced that progress was a sham—yet Christianity marked him profoundly. The destructive force of evil, degradation, the wretchedness of man alone are present throughout his work, but transfigured by the warmth and sensuality of his palette. With Delacroix, color is a form of redemption. *Christ on the Cross* in the Vannes Museum, *Christ in the Tomb* in Boston, not to mention the series of *Christ on the Lake of Gennesaret*, bear witness to a fairly rare feeling for the evangelical message.

The audience listens to me politely. A few coughs and the slight creaking of chairs warn me that it is time to make way for the music. I go and sit in one of the stalls near the altar. At least I have kept to my allotted time, timing being the main principle of all gatherings these days, whether it be a seminar, convention, round table, sermon, plenum, or garden party. Timing forms the basis of all modern collective activities. It's the stopwatch that counts, not the content.

I have not gone beyond the time allowed: three minutes. The first item comes from *The Well-Tempered Clavier* by Johann Sebastian Bach, which can be played on any type of keyboard. Saint-Sulpice has played an important part in the revival of the cantor, thanks to Albert Schweitzer who came and played Bach here at the beginning of the century.

The organ at Saint-Sulpice is in much more original condition than the one in Notre Dame, which has been mutilated by various kinds of tinkering intended to increase the virtuosity of the player. The instrument with its sixty-four stops, designed by Clicquot in 1781, rapidly became famous throughout Europe. As we know, the great organ builder Cavaillé-Coll rebuilt it when Delacroix was painting the Chapel of the Holy Angels. With one hundred stops spread over five keyboards, the organist's hands and feet can set no fewer than seven thousand pipes vibrating.

From Nivers and Clérambault, the title of organist at Saint-Sulpice has always been awarded to eminent musicians like Charles-Marie Widor, who loved to take part in musical contests with Gabriel Fauré at the choir organ. There is a subtle harmony of proportion and grandeur between the church and this seven-tiered instrument in its stone case.

I found out that there was a mysterious third organ from the Trianon that had belonged to the Dauphin, the son of Louis XV. Sold at auction during the Revolution, it was picked up by the parish priest of Saint-Sulpice in 1804 when Pope Pius VII came to Paris for Napoleon's coronation and visited the church. In 1926 this organ was stored behind the door with Delacroix's *Heliodorus* above it. It is a dark corner, although less so when the painter was working on the Holy Angels. The buildings put up when Baron Haussmann redesigned Paris subsequently took away a lot of light.

A new interlude. The parish priest came and whispered to me during the Bach: "Don't forget to say something about *Wrestling with the Angel*...the significance of the spiritual struggle." There is something inflexible yet good-humored about this priest. He has an aura of calm authority, so different from the despotic parish priest of my childhood. He looks both earnest and lively: a real leader of souls in the tradition of the men of Saint-Sulpice.

We have often discussed the meaning of *Wrestling with the Angel*. He wonders about it. A sentence in the *Journal* dated 1822 intrigues him: "There is something in me that is stronger than my body.... If only all the soul had to fight was the body!" He hesitates about the meaning that should be ascribed to the two painting in the Holy Angels. "Did he want to acknowledge that at the end of the day one could not escape being marked by God? Did he want to show that one day, at the end of the struggle, one had to recognize God and, like Jacob, ask for His blessing?" He refuses to decide one way or the other.

I feel as if I am experiencing a unique, privileged moment, but perhaps it may also be a kind of deception. Am I not taking someone else's place? I know that laymen are taking an increasing part in worship, and that they are in the same position as I am when they come up to read passages from the Old Testament or from the epistles of Saint Paul.

But this evening it's Delacroix. Like all great painters, the master has given rise to a set of beliefs and practices associated with his name that have an element of worship, with its clergy, its faithful, and its bigots. Does this religion have more priests than parishioners? Moreover this liturgy is practiced only at anniversaries in the form of ceremonies: exhibitions, folio editions, lectures. I am aware of being an intruder; at the same time, it has been instilled into me since childhood that a church legitimates and sanctifies one's words. That no doubt explains the feeling of being a usurper. Still, I quite like having secularized worship for a few moments.

I sit down feeling quite exhausted as the first notes of *Wrestling with the Angel* ring out. It's very soft, yet contains a power that grows to a fury. I imagine it is describing the fight—recognition, then bodies feeling and reaching out for each other in the dark but without violence. As in judo, this exercise requires more technique than strength, the point of the combat being to down or immobilize one's adversary.

Listening to the music I am struck by the title. One always says wrestling *with* the angel, never wrestling *against* the angel. I had never thought of that. Wrestling is always against someone. So there is some secret connivance in this barehanded contest. Jacob and the angel are colluding. However, the game is not rigged. That is the elusive, hidden aspect of this duel. After all Jacob risks death ("I have seen God face to face, and my life is preserved"). Everything is in the grip and the thrust to destabilize the adversary. Some translators who follow the text of Genesis very closely don't hesitate to use the term *boxing match*.[3] The tightrope walker was right: losing balance is fatal.

The piece inspires a series of harmonizing and opposing feelings: mystery, night, the frenzy of a wild struggle, both stillness and movement. The composer has interrupted the music with moments of dramatic silence symbolizing the semistillness of the angel. I can feel emotion in the audience; it is palpable even from where I am sitting. It vibrates and comes in waves not necessarily following the flow of the music rising from the organ. The harmony rises and falls more quickly now like a mounting sea suddenly sending the waves crashing into each other. Then the violence slowly subsides and the final passage describes the calm of dawn when the fight ends.

The lecturer comes up to me at the exit in her usual caustic style. She always has this irritating mixture of provocation and approval. This evening she really has surpassed herself in Sulpician chic: a spiky necklace, big cuffs, black leather jacket, and blood red lips! She looks me straight in the eye and, as if she had guessed what I was thinking, declares:

"You mentioned that Sade was baptized in this church. But you could also have made some reference to Delacroix's sadism!"

"Was this really the time and place? Besides, it's a rather worn-out theme. Baudelaire, whom you love to quote so much, has said everything there is to say on that subject. Bataille—you must like Bataille—said that Delacroix's painting is linked to the representation of death."

"There you are!" she exclaims triumphantly.

"He was speaking of his work in general. I don't really think that Bataille's definition applies to *Jacob Wrestling with the Angel*."

"That's possible. In any case, Delacroix died once the painting was finished."

"That's not quite true. There was a period of two years between. He never recovered from that labor, nor perhaps also from the mixed reception it received. Anyway, I can't see the image of death in *Wrestling with the Angel*. On the contrary, it depicts life. The world's first heartbeats. The dawn of creation. *Heliodorus* is different. The profanation of the Temple with man on the ground is the test of truth: dread, death, a world gone wrong."

Our conversation has brought us close to the Chapel of the Holy Angels. It is difficult to avoid it when leaving the church. At this hour, when night has fallen some time ago, the floodlights throw a blinding light on the two mural paintings. These opposing spotlights distort the perception of the two panels. It would have been better to position them away from the window so that they at least respect the angle of the light coming from outside. That is the way Delacroix wanted it and, even if the *Journal* does not mention the subject, it is likely that full sunlight made his task more difficult. This is the reason why painters usually choose their studios to the north.

We stop outside the Chapel of the Souls in Purgatory. The lecturer lowers her voice and confides to me:

"This chapel is disturbing. The paintings on the wall look like ghosts. I avoid this place, in spite of myself."

"You're right. They are only shadows now."

"Yes, the kingdom of shadows, the nether world. That's how I imagine the infernal powers, Hades."

"It's dedicated to the Souls in Purgatory...."

"I know that," she replies testily. "I was speaking of the underworld in mythology, not the Christian Hell for the damned."

The sacristan asks the stragglers to leave.

"I'm locking up now or I'll lock you in," he said.

I admit I was afraid that she might say, "Try it, I dare you!"

CHAPTER 11

Maigret in the Argonne

A quiet little village in France, full of flowers. The cornfields come right up to the houses lining the only street. Contault-le-Maupas, an indeterminate commune in the Argonne, on the border between the wet and the chalky areas of Champagne, is no more than a string of half-timbered brick houses. One can tell a dying village from the lack of people in the streets and the fact that the forecourt of the church has been converted to parking space. As in many small rural towns, the presence of charming window boxes and pretty flower beds in front of the houses makes up for the disappearance of shops and businesses.

These village flower displays are no doubt intended to show that although there is not much going on, the town still has lively residents who have no intention of leaving. But where are they? Contault as a village is like many others, but it is also bewildering. One could say that it has "great metaphysical beauty," like a painting by de Chirico. The pediment of the church bears the date 1825, the only beacon linking the present and the past. These unexplained figures make me think of the stopped hands on a clock painted by that painter of dreams—another artist haunted by the figure of a father who had died prematurely! Contault, with its seventy inhabitants, is a few miles from Givry-en-Argonne, the birthplace of the Delacroix family.

In 1776, after his patron Turgot fell from favor, Charles

Delacroix acquired a property known as the Château de Contault and called himself Charles de Lacroix de Contault. This, however, did not prevent him standing at the election for the new Département de la Marne as "a Contault farmer." Perhaps he thought that buying a farm in the region in 1791 would justify this occupation.

In 1792 he was elected as a deputy to the convention. Through bad spelling, Contault becomes first Contaut then Constant. This double name follows him for some time. When he voted for the king's death in 1792, it was in the name of Delacroix de Constant. As secretary of the National Convention, he took part in the Declaration of the Rights of Man. Among the many positions he held, we should remember that of the commissioner in charge of auctioning the furniture from the Petit Trianon, which had belonged to Queen Marie-Antoinette.

In the end, not a great deal is known about the personality of this man who rose to the highest positions in the state: he was minister of Foreign Affairs in the Directoire, prefect of the Bouches-du-Rhône, then of the Gironde under the Empire. His career is typical of the provincial bourgeoisie that served its apprenticeship under the Ancien Régime and was given significant administrative power during the Revolution. He was clever and determined, a man of some character as evidenced by the stoicism he showed during his operation. His ready acceptance of a less prestigious post in Holland after his dismissal indicates that he could also eat humble pie. These are the few characteristics we can glean about him.

Eugène did not have much time to know his father, who was seventeen years older than his mother and died in 1805. In his *Journal*, he recalls his father with filial piety and admiration: "Think of your father and conquer your natural irresponsibility! Don't be nice to people who have few scruples."

*   *   *

Do Delacroix's origins justify this trip to the Argonne? Surely not. I often question the rather suspect ties I am always trying to weave with the past. What I admire in Maigret is not the policeman but the patient hunter of clues. There is no one better than this deeply placid, portly inspector who soaks up not only beer in the bar, but also sounds, colors, and noises. I love the good-natured wisdom of the character, and the idea of haunting the scene of the crime to nose it out and make it talk. An apparently insignificant detail picked up by Maigret is always the sign that something has clicked. With Maigret, it's not just a question of the guilty party coming clean; things and objects also have to confess, not as proof in the manner of Sherlock Holmes, but as if they had a soul, or at the very least a history or a destiny.

Eugène Delacroix had the same relationship with the material world: "I want the place I inhabit, the objects I use, to speak to me of what they have seen, what they have been and what was with them."

It goes without saying that there was never any murder connected with the family committed at Contault, but I have to breathe the atmosphere of this village to understand the beginnings of "the family novel." Here I am once again giving in to my obsession, making my devotions to the past. I am fascinated by the way events that happened long ago are linked. It's always the same story of tracing paternity in time gone by!

My search in the Argonne began with a very Simenon-style impregnation in a Sainte-Menehould inn, just as Maigret likes them. There was a smell of sawdust and hearty cooking, the window panes were steamed up and some locals were whispering earnestly and quietly in a corner.

The Argonne is the scene of King Louis XVIth's capture at Varennes, the battle of Valmy, and fierce fighting in 1915. It is a

region of France whose land is marked with more than its share
of scars and stigmata. They are visible even in the trees (the
famous "machine-gunned wood," bits of exploded shells), and
they certainly speak of loss and destruction, but in the manner of
living, familiar signs. They don't refer to death; on the contrary,
they are evidence of resistance and energy. I hope to discover
some sign of the vibrancy of these traces in Contault.

What can be revealed by a village where the painter probably
never set foot, either on his first visit to the château in 1856 or in
1859? Finding evidence of a nonexistent visit is an enterprise
that cannot fail. Nothing has disappeared, since no mark was left
in the first place. Anything can happen: a piece of information, a
chance meeting, a trail to follow. There is an old hunting term,
connaissances, referring to the footprint of the animal being
hunted. I am convinced that it is impossible for people to live and
leave no *connaissances*. One always leaves some trace behind, be
it ever so tiny, which will be found whenever the determined
instinct of the hunter is applied to the task. Charles Delacroix de
Contault at least left a clue: that double-barreled name. He
owned a property and a house in this locality. There must be
ruins or at least a site.

I wander down la Grand-Rue, the main and only street, listening for a sound that would give me some chance of getting my
bearings, but there is nothing apart from the gust of wind blowing down between the two lines of hills overlooking the village.
"Do you think there is anyone living here?" queries my wife
Joëlle, who has come with me to the Argonne. The only dwelling
that looks as if it belongs to someone of any note is situated at the
entrance to the little town. It is a solid brick building with elegant
arched carriage doors. The shutters are padlocked, the garden is
well kept. I catch sight of the town hall. It is closed. There is,

however, a bulletin board giving the home address of the mayor.

He lives in a house with splendid cosmos in bloom. I ring the bell. A tall, good-looking blonde woman opens the door. Who am I? A door-to-door salesman? A petty thief? Pilfering could be an accurate enough way of describing what I am doing. Wandering about the countryside looking for a clue or a feeling is something like sentimental poaching. Believing that revelation will come from an impression.... Basically, it's a form of laziness: letting yourself be carried along by impulse and sensation. It's less tiring to feel than to think.

"May I speak to the mayor? He does live here?"

"He does indeed," the woman says with a smile.

A lively-looking young man with big bright eyes hurries up carrying a hammer in his hand.

"I'm the mayor. How may I help you?" he asks good-naturedly.

I explain the aim of my visit in a few words even though I don't really know it myself, but under certain circumstances I must confess that I have a matchless ability to give a clarity to the vagueness of what I am doing. He finds my trip to Contault quite a natural thing. He knows about Charles Delacroix's Argonne origins, but also his links with the commune.

"Come in. I'm doing some odd jobs. It's Saturday," he says excusing himself.

When he pays a visit, Inspector Maigret sits himself down whether invited to or not, so that the person to whom he is speaking understands that he is not someone who can be got rid of in a few minutes. I do the same, not to imitate him but to be able to take notes more comfortably.

A double ladder is propped up against the sitting room wall, which is full of sea pictures quite delicately done.

"It's my wife. It reminds her of her native Brittany. Contault obviously has nothing to do with the sea. In winter it's sometimes a bit dismal."

He tells me that in Eugène Delacroix's time there were almost three hundred inhabitants in Contault, whereas today there are hardly seventy. He calls on Joëlle to bear witness to that.

"We comprise only ten farmers. Peasants here are a dying race. And we have just three holiday houses."

I bring up the subject of Charles Delacroix's property. He situates the farm in the main street, but not the château.

"Look. I'd like to know that myself. I haven't been able to identify this château, or the house they call a château. There's the site of a Templars' Château as you leave the village, but it doesn't correspond to Charles Delacroix's."

"Wouldn't it be the fairly solid brick building at the entrance to Contault?" I ask.

"I thought of that. It could be something like it....It's the biggest house in the village. It was bought by some Dutch people. But there's nothing to show that it was the property of Charles Delacroix."

"You must have archives at the Town Hall."

"Nothing at all. As you can imagine, I've looked. It was before the Revolution. There's nothing left of all that."

I feel that I'm going to return empty-handed from my journey to the Argonne. He senses my disappointment.

"I suppose you know Paul Loppin?"

Loppin, Loppin...Ah yes! I remember. It was at the Château de Crozes near Souillac. The lady of the house had told me that a judge of the Supreme Court of Appeal had gone to see her and had explored the family archives. Although it had apparently yielded nothing new, my visit to Crozes had put me on the track of François-Joseph Heim, Delacroix's neighbor in Saint-Sulpice. I am convinced that all these threads that interlace create a central motif. I remember that the lady of the manor had told me that Monsieur Loppin had found some extremely important letters written by Charles Delacroix.

"Did you know that Paul Loppin has published several booklets on Charles Delacroix? Have you looked at them?"

"I must admit I haven't. Should I?"

"It's very interesting. I managed to get hold of them, as Contault is mentioned quite a lot. I'll show them to you."

The mayor returns with several small books. These studies published by Pierre Béarn are often quoted in bibliographies. René Huyghe, author of the masterly *Delacroix ou le Combat solitaire*, while not entirely rejecting the Talleyrand theory, refers to Paul Loppin's research in an appendix. At the end of the enquiry, it would appear that Eugène Delacroix was simply born prematurely and that Charles was indeed the father.

"You'll find everything in this booklet. The letters between Charles and his wife Victoire, who was expecting Eugène when her husband was posted to Holland, are published in it."

"I must say you're awfully well informed!"

"Because of Contault," he says, almost apologetically. "As mayor, one has to take an interest in the history of the commune."

My hostess at Crozes had talked about this discovery, especially the fact that the affectionate tone Charles Delacroix used was not that of a deceived husband. I had cast something of a chill by replying that such sentiments did not prove anything.

I skim through the booklet the mayor handed to me, pausing at a letter written on 2 February 1798. It strongly gives the lie to those who claim that Charles Delacroix was quite ignorant of his wife's pregnancy when he left to take up his posting at the Hague. Not only did he know about it, but he advised Victoire against coming to Holland as she intended. "You must wait at least until the roads and the season are better," Charles recommends, "which," Loppin notes, "indicates at least the definite appearance of spring; whence it is logical to deduce that the birth is not expected in the first weeks of spring." Moreover, Loppin points out that if Mme. Delacroix had been an unfaithful wife, she would never have considered going to Holland and "presenting her husband with the ever-increasing evidence of a pregnancy more advanced than it should be."

All these facts are convincing, I admit, but they still do not comprise indisputable proof. Besides, Paul Loppin admits it implicitly. He produces a letter of 19 April 1798, which, according to him, is conclusive evidence. It is written by Mme. Delacroix and contains the following passage: "I am still suffering from the strain I had getting into the carriage coming back from Paris. It does not restrict me completely, but I have trouble walking. I do hope that there will be no repercussions from it."

For Paul Loppin, these lines provide the key to the mystery: Victoire Oeben hopes that the sudden movement she made in the carriage will have no future consequences. "Well indeed there is one!" Loppin writes triumphantly. "It is exactly a week later, on 7 Floreal Year VI, in other words 26 April 1798, when Ferdinand Victor Eugène is born!!!" The future painter was a premature baby.

While I am sitting on the sofa busily taking notes, the master of the house is up on his ladder hammering nails into the wall. A child is sitting on a chair quietly reading a comic. Joëlle is looking at the sea paintings. A studious atmosphere occasionally interrupted by gusts of wind blowing under the door. I could have gone to the Bibliothèque Nationale to look at this book, but it had to be discovered here at Contault, as if to show that a disciple of Jules Maigret is always rewarded in the end.

Nevertheless, one must admit that in spite of Paul Loppin's shouts of victory, these elements do not irrefutably prove Charles Delacroix's paternity, even if it is a very strong probability. The likelihood of a premature baby of seven, indeed six months, surviving in those days is difficult to imagine. Indeed some specialists have noticed the fact that, a few days after the birth, the child was feeding normally.[1] "Her milk is flowing well," the mother writes, which is hardly compatible with a premature baby. These same specialists tend, therefore, to favor a normal pregnancy, and thus accept that Charles Delacroix could father a child before his operation. On the other hand, there is no serious fact, only a vague resemblance, to support the case for Talleyrand who, as it happens, never claimed to be the father.

In the 1960s Camille Bernard, a passionate admirer of Delacroix, had patiently gathered together documents relating to the painter. He told René Huyghe, who quotes him, that he had discovered the identity of Delacroix's real father. Bernard died in 1998. All his archives were dispersed and sold by his heirs.

The mayor looks at me with some amusement.

"Now I think you have everything you need."

"All the same, this question of the house is frustrating. Perhaps Charles Delacroix never lived in Contault, and just received the income from his farm."

"No, he did have a house. I'm sure of it. He lived in Contault and I can prove it. A brother of the painter was born here. Here, I have a copy of the birth certificate."

He hands me a document: Henry Delacroix was born on 12 June 1787 in Contault. He died on 14 June 1807 in Friedland.

Henry Delacroix is another matter that I have not been able to clear up. His brother Eugène never mentions him in his *Journal*, whereas he often writes about Charles-Henry, a general and baron of the Empire, aide-de-camp to Prince Eugène. He died in 1845. It was traditionally claimed in the family that the two brothers, Charles-Henry and Henry, met on the evening of the victory at Friedland. They fell into each other's arms. A few moments later Henry was killed by a cannonball. Now, it has been established that Charles-Henry did not take part in the Battle of Friedland. Poor Henry was only twenty when he died. We talk with the mayor about Friedland, the scene of a hopeless defeat of the Russian army, crushed by Napoleon in only a few hours.

"What a pity to die at twenty so far from home," says the mayor, "especially after winning the battle."

Why do I feel this sudden urge to tell him that a few years ago I actually visited the Friedland battlefield, about eighteen miles from Eylau? I feel I am among people I can trust. There is an atmosphere of kindness and calm that encourages the dropping of inhibitions. I explain to him that Friedland and Eylau, formerly places in Eastern Prussia, are now part of the Russian enclave of Kaliningrad. The event—"that dust," as Fernand Braudel called it—has also left its mark in the former German province. The spirit of the past has settled everywhere, against the wishes of the Russians who, after 1945, tried to destroy all traces of anything German. While talking to the mayor, I suddenly think of that dust. It can never be got rid of. It covers the walls of ruined churches, the roads lined with old lime trees, which still have bits of paving from the German period.

Why, in Contault, should my thoughts turn to that quality of silence, the dreamy melancholy of that open country crossed by streams and ditches? In Friedland I had the impression of travelling during the 1930s, when the roads were empty and people went on foot, walking on the side of the road. The sky seemed vast and the trees enormous. I have never found dust so fine and clinging in any other landscape.

"If you want to find Contault's dust, you really have to look for it," the mayor says with a laugh.

"Oh, but I'm not leaving empty-handed."

"It's true. In our part of the world, you have to scour the countryside to find what you want," he says with a hint of pride in his voice. "Our name requires it."

"What name?"

"Contault. Apparently it comes from the Latin, *conditus*, hidden. We make a point of keeping things to ourselves. Go to Givry," he suggests with a boyish smile.

"Givry? Is there some trace of the Delacroix family?"

"You'll see it in the main street. At least there's a plaque. That's more than we have."

Joëlle and I leave Contault with some regret: the peace of the village deep in the valley, the long shadows and the geometrical shapes they form, auspicious indications that I think I noticed and like to believe in. A quest needs good omens. The mayor's welcome and the discovery of Paul Loppin seem to me like signs from heaven. They confirm my belief in the effectiveness of the Simenon method.

On leaving the village I find myself feeling strangely disconsolate, as if I had confided something precious to Contault. "Maigret in Delacroix country." What would he do in a case like this? The inspector is a man with a lot of good sense. Before prowling around Delacroix, he would ask: "What is the problem?" But how could I explain to him what is at stake with *Jacob*

Wrestling with the Angel, its elusive origin, and the mystery contained in the wall of the Holy Angels? He would certainly investigate the surroundings.

Disturbing coincidences arise, especially from 1855, the year when Delacroix seriously tackles *Wrestling with the Angel*. He feels a frantic need to travel, wanting to visit his numerous cousins. In 1856 he goes to Givry-en-Argonne. He had never been there. The painter is anxious to visit Charles Delacroix's house. He meditates beside his paternal grandmother's grave. He is touched to meet a distant cousin who bears his name. As a bachelor he seems reassured to know that the family name is in no danger of dying out.

This trip takes place in the very same year that the story of his doubtful birth is brought up for the first time by the art critic Théophile Silvestre, even though he only alludes to it. This would tend to prove that the gossip was definitely being spread in certain circles. This was also the time when Delacroix's varicocele reappears. This painful condition of the testicles recalls his father's famous tumor. It is a way of Eugène saying to Charles: "Father, why have you abandoned me?" It can therefore be compared with Jacob's trial when his hip is dislocated. Biblical scholars see a sexual allusion in this: the hip for the groin, an indirect way of indicating the penis.

Givry today still forms a kind of promontory overlooking a plain crossed by forests, streams, and ponds. There is indeed a plaque on the wall of a butcher shop in the main street, bearing this inscription: "Part of the house where Delacroix, a member of the National Convention and father of the famous painter, was born." I admire their concern with precision: this portion of the dwelling with its corrugated iron roof looks a modest dwelling indeed. In the village there is also a street called rue Delacroix after "a Givry family." I appreciate the simplicity of the inscription. This commune does not make a great fuss over its local celebrities. Charles Delacroix's father was a bailiff employed by the Comte de Belval, Bishop of Rennes, the person of note in the area. He administered the Argonne properties and had twelve children, eight of whom survived. The painter's innumerable cousins came from Charles' six sisters. Charles was the eldest of the family.

There is something impermeable in this land of the Argonne. Apart from its ability to withstand water, its mystery comes from an interior force that allows superficial contact but never really reveals itself.

I don't think that the Argonne has any particularly determining effect on its inhabitants. The geography of the place does not explain anything, but its ability to keep its secrets sums up Delacroix's inaccessible character well. In the 1920s, it was decided to plant spruce in the Haute-Chevauchée forest, where the bloodiest battles of the Argonne took place. Nothing grew under the shroud of pine needles that covered the forest floor, so that many traces of the war have been left intact: bunkers, trenches, guns, shells. The Argonne, the only forest in France where tree stumps are never burned.... The risk of explosions is too great.

It would certainly be taking things too far to say that a certain Argonne distrust had marked Delacroix's temperament. Nevertheless, it pleases me to see an endurance and invulnerability in him, which is also a form of resistance. Delacroix is always the opponent, the aggressor, impenetrable.

These characteristics are recognizable in the stranger who attacks Jacob during the night of the Jabbok crossing.

CHAPTER 12

A Night in Saint-Sulpice

Spring 1996. The organ is playing the theme of the *Dies Irae*, the piece from the Mass for the Dead that Delacroix liked so much. "Day of wrath... " No doubt he felt at home in that atmosphere of anger and desolation. It is eleven o'clock at night....During the pauses, the muffled sounds of the city slip into the church so softly that they almost seem to brush it. Now and again I think I hear the more urgent noise of the eighty-six bus. The sounds of horns and brakes arrive like fading echoes and are immediately swallowed up by the voice of the organ.

I am shut in the church. The Chapel of the Holy Angels is brilliantly lit. I have never seen *Jacob Wrestling with the Angel* lit by the floodlights look so dazzling. The darkness outside emphasizes the blinding, harsh, almost fierce intensity of the wall. It is a garish, unnatural light, which changes the balance of the painting as a whole, making relief and contrast disappear. The three huge trees shimmer and seem to be slowly waving their heavy branches. The part with the shepherds and flocks, already glowing without this artificial light, now shines too brightly. Only the angel and Jacob seem to be still.

I am shut in but I am not alone. A film crew is busy around me. The director has the necessary authorizations to film the chapel in peace at night. He has used the occasion to ask the organist at Saint-Sulpice to play the pieces that Delacroix liked.

I came to know the filmmaker by chance when I read an article about one of his films called *La Blessure de Jacob* [*Jacob's Wound*]. I soon learned that the subject concerned *Jacob Wrestling with the Angel*, not by Delacroix but by Rembrandt—the picture is in the Staatlische Museum in Berlin. After vainly trying to find the cassette, in the end I contacted the director. At our first interview he had grilled me about Delacroix's painting without appearing to do so. I can become very talkative on this subject.

The director is one of those reflective, very observant people who let you talk while they look as if their minds are elsewhere. But they take in everything. At the time I had not been on my guard against those dark eyes I thought were wandering, but were actually seeing right into me. At the end of the conversation he suggested that I make a film with him on the *Wrestling with the Angel* in Saint-Sulpice. I was taken by surprise and tried to give him countless reasons for me to refuse. "I write books for the very reason that I can't talk about them." It is true that words often betray me, unless it is I who lie to them. My arguments amused him. I was wasting my breath. I told him that I would think it over, which is a polite way of refusing by putting it off. In the meantime I saw his film on Rembrandt. I was won over by his subtlety and discretion, revealing the development of the Flemish artist with rare depth. Rembrandt painted that picture at a moment of crisis in his life when he had lost his wife and children, and his house and goods had been sold off at auction.

Rembrandt has depicted an embrace rather than a fight. The erotic element is quite evident. Jacob seems to be struggling; the look in the angel's eyes, however, is fondly protective, and he even goes so far as to stroke his neck. It would seem to have nothing in common with Delacroix. Yet the two scenes are alike, even if the sensual element is less transparent in the Chapel of the

Holy Angels. I have often been intrigued by the Angel's relaxed, almost langorous pose. I was aware of what Claudel had written: "These two bodies in violent embrace, the extreme sculpting of bones and muscles pressed together, becoming aware of each other (heart against heart and mouth against mouth—throughout the night that it lasted!...)"[1]

Claudel is not the only one to notice the femininity of the angel attacked by a determined, vigorous young man. Jacques Audiberti puts it more crudely when he notes that this angel is "groping Jacob in a strange way. He boldly moulds the palm of his hand over the bulging thigh muscle, his fingers feeling for the nerve to make it freeze. When you come to think of it, there is something dry, more precisely 'dehydrated,'[2] in the overall tone of the fresco."

Did Delacroix know Rembrandt's painting? It is likely, as there were prints in circulation. Anyway, what does it matter! Many artists have depicted this episode from Genesis as a "mystical dance,"[3] others as an amorous encounter. A stall in Cordoba Cathedral has a panel showing Jacob and the angel in a seduction scene.

When Delacroix was beginning his work at Saint-Sulpice, another French painter, Paul Baudry, was finishing a *Jacob Wrestling with the Angel* at the Villa Medici. No one ever mentions this painting, which today hangs in the Museum of La Roche-sur-Yon. The man to whom we owe the decorations in the foyer of the Opéra can be considered a representative of the pompous style as much as you like, but he was the first nineteenth-century artist to tackle this theme. And that is no small thing! He finished this picture in 1853. This was well before Delacroix, even though he had chosen the subject in 1850. The stance of the two figures in Baudry's painting is very close to

Rembrandt's. Jacob's nudity, the way he grasps the angel and holds him between his thighs while the other struggles feebly could be considered indecent. It is not very far from rape. It certainly shocked people at the time. Baudry tried to sell it without success, and ended up donating it to the town where he was born.

Rembrandt and Baudry: I'm thinking of these two painters this evening as I look at Delacroix's *Wrestling with the Angel*. The commentator in the film on Rembrandt quotes the painter Jean Bazaine (he also did a *Jacob Wrestling with the Angel*): "It's the painting that looks at us."

While the scaffolding and lighting are being installed so that the smallest detail of the painting can be filmed, I look at *Wrestling with the Angel* looking at me. It's clear that it has been observing me from the beginning. I have never stopped being overpowered by it. This painting steals away a part of myself. It dominates me; I am in its thrall. I didn't choose the prison of the Holy Angels. I was simply put inside before I knew it, like an idiot. One does not escape from a jail that has no bars or warders.

This evening I enter the surrounding walls once again and willingly put my name in the prison register. I suppose I must like it; I must enjoy staying in the Holy Angels cell. Prisoners never tire of looking at the walls of their dungeon.

For me walls do not symbolize being shut away; on the contrary, they represent freedom. I had the power to imagine what I liked on the cracked surface with its damp stains. It is beyond the jailers' control, but the control the prisoner has over this screen can be absolute. It is the planisphere where the height of his hopes and the depths of despair are projected and measured. A wall is no obstacle to a prisoner; it belongs to him. In fact this wall chart defies the warder.

My fascination with Delacroix and the Holy Angels owes a lot to the way the painter battled against the wall. Immured in Saint-Sulpice, he was digging a tunnel for at least seven years. It was like working in the hold of a ship. "I have made a solid effort. I think it will save the work, which was probably bogged down," he confides to Berryer in October 1858. A bog, mud, the feeling of getting lost and sinking into the ground. Let us not forget the verse from the Psalms over the entrance to the chapel he decorated: "Deliver me out of the mire, and let me not sink."

One July day in 1861 he came out into the light again. To say that he worked in obscurity is not a figure of speech. Delacroix battled against the daylight. The constant movements of the sky made life difficult for him. He does not refer to it in his *Journal*. It is likely that the window was blocked out by a curtain. The painter opened and shut it according to the position of the sun, as if adjusting the aperture in a camera.

The cameraman adjusts a mobile crane so that he can photograph *Wrestling with the Angel* from the front. The mural paintings occupy a dominating position in relation to the person looking at them. You have always had to raise your eyes to study them. From another distance and height, the eye sees a different *Jacob Wrestling with the Angel*. Delacroix has played with the semicircular vaults, which echo the shape of the foliage on the three trees, spreading a protective shade over the whole scene.

No one has climbed up to the ceiling apart from the painter himself, his assistant Andrieu, and no doubt the people who did the restoration work in the 1970s. I was forgetting the photographer for Maurice Sérullaz's book *Peintures murales*, who captured many details of *Wrestling with the Angel* at the beginning of the 1960s.

While the technicians are laying the cables and setting up the lights, I make my way up to the organ loft. The organist is playing Prelude No. 2 by Chopin, the composer who was so dear to Delacroix. "He is the truest artist I have met."

I very quietly come up to the console. The organist has not seen me. The keyboard and all the stops are in the shape of an amphitheater. In the center, the musician's fingers seem to be doing battle. They charge, mingle in a hand-to-hand fight, retreat then launch another assault. Actually, it is more like ballet than a fight. There is an aspect that is supple, free, and arranged like a dance in these well-ordered waves of attack. Chopin's music adds a daring, acrobatic dimension to the exercise.

The organist sees me and stops suddenly. I urge him to continue, but he wants to do the honors and show me the instrument. I notice that the case in the shape of an ancient temple is topped by two angels holding out a lyre. There is a phenomenal number of celestial creatures per square foot in this church. They are in nooks and crannies everywhere. I discover two other groups of three little angels on each side of the pediment. The angel on the left is standing on the very edge with his hand raised in triumph. He has a mischievous air about him and looks ready to leap into the choir.

The organist explains how the organ works. He lightly touches some keys: the effect gives an extraordinary fullness to the crescendo followed by a diminuendo or distancing effect when the valve is closed.

"This organ was restored in the nineteenth century, but that doesn't make it a romantic instrument. The classical tradition and the romantic revival are intimately connected. This link is very much in the spirit of Cavaillé-Coll. The organ at Saint-Sulpice is admired throughout the world."

He plays a few notes, which pierce the silence. It is like a shock, cutting very sharply and cleanly into the depths of the night.

"The acoustics at Saint-Sulpice are neither too generous nor too dry. The sound travels for about six seconds. The tall organ case sometimes tends to block the sound, stops it from spreading. But between you and me, that's insignificant compared with the greatness and refinement of the instrument."

"What is your reaction to knowing that it played a role in *Jacob Wrestling with the Angel?*"

He looks thoughtful, then a little smile appears at the corners of his mouth.

"The chapel and the organ loft are so close. The door to the stairs adjoins the Holy Angels. There is a real complicity between the two. What part did this music play in Delacroix's inspiration? It's obviously impossible to say...."

The sounds of the city seem to be farther and farther away. The smell of the empty church enfolded by night has changed. It is heavier, as if the absence of light had dulled the fresh fragrances of day. It is something like the heady, slightly fusty smell of precious old wood, probably from the stearin in the candles, the fatty acid that attracts dust and blackens the stone in churches. The shadows and diminishing sounds can modify odors: the olfactory nerve is no longer distracted by other sensations, and becomes more acute.

I have to go down into the church again. The organ has begun a solemn melody that echoes all through the building—no doubt a *Te Deum*. A hurricane of sound descends on Saint-Sulpice. In the darkness a polyphonic ten on the Beaufort wind scale rises in a succession of foaming waves, then suddenly the storm dies down and a fragile solo voice rises into the air: it is a melody by Louis-Nicolas Clérambault, an organist at Saint-Sulpice in the eighteenth century.

Before going back to the Chapel of the Holy Angels, I walk around the side aisles, borne along by this riverlike course surrounding the nave, the only part of Saint-Sulpice to win Huysmans' approval. ("You could cleanse your soul without being seen; you felt at home.")[4] The closed chapel where the Marquis de Sade was christened seems like a deserted shore.

I cannot help thinking about all the famous voices that have echoed beneath these vaults. Camille Desmoulins' wedding and those words of Robespierre, his best man, addressed to his friend: "Don't cry, you hypocrite." And the banquet for seven thousand guests given in this very place in honor of Bonaparte on his return from Egypt (6 November 1799), with the crowd applauding and admiring the escort of "Africans of Egypt," while the last member of the Couperin dynasty played patriotic songs on the organ! It was a strange dinner: the guests were keeping a strict watch on each other. That evening Bonaparte decided to try his luck. Three days later came the coup d'état of the 18 Brumaire.... Victor Hugo saying "I do" to Adèle Foucher in the Chapel of the Holy Virgin.... Jacques Prévert as an altar boy making the responses at mass in Latin. He later wrote a poem called "Le Combat avec l'Ange," which is very anti-Catholic.

Have these sleeping ghosts of words left any trace on the walls or the stones? Will a discovery one day enable us to bring them to life again? Who could have predicted that a layer of magnetic oxide on a tape could re-create sounds that had long disappeared? What was Bossuet's voice like, for example? He preached at least twice in Saint-Sulpice. He must have said his r's from the back of the throat like a peasant from the Berry or a Québecois from Montreal. All the court spoke like that at the time. The word for king [roi] was pronounced rway instead of rwa. We would be shocked today by the sacred orator's rustic speech, so inappropriate to the nobility of the thought he was expressing.

The church at night may seem deserted and silent, but it

seethes with life. The paintings, blackened with dirt and damp, appear to have grown on the walls like rhizomes. Despite the dull flakes peeling off the surface, these murals still survive. They have the charm of shady paths overgrown by trees and the melancholy of old local roads no longer traveled. The damp has put a bloom on the walls; the stone is burgeoning. As they lose their pigment, the colors have developed granulation reminiscent of flower jardinières, ivies, or plants with tendrils clinging to corner walls that receive only dim waves of light from outside.

It is easy to scoff at these edifying paintings with their dead colors, and to compare them unfavorably with the two panels by Delacroix. At least his colleagues worked away at their particular jobs, choosing subjects that were easy to understand: an episode in the life of a saint here, a historical anecdote there. Signol, Landelle, and Glaize are so alike in their concern with didactic simplicity that in the end one cannot tell them apart. They had modest aims and results that matched: mediocre. Delacroix, on the other hand, quite consciously commits the sin of pride.

The organ is playing a very gentle work by César Franck, which seems to bring peace to the night in Saint-Sulpice. This whole open area populated with candlesticks, chairs, benches, and confessionals seems to have been subdued. Even the shadows look softer. Languet de Gergy's mausoleum is the only thing that remains as disturbing as ever. Death is fleeing before immortality, but it is still terrifying. Whatever the sculptor intended, this mocking skeleton is not giving in without a fight, writhing like a devil as he waves his scythe. Diderot is very severe in his judgment when he writes that "taken as a whole, this piece of sculpture does not attract attention," and that "it does not have the harmony, the silence, and the peace monuments of this kind should possess." Personally, I find this blending of marble and bronze in the style of Bernini very expressive. It is one of the many unusual features of the church.

Saint-Sulpice is like the projection, on a monumental scale, of the church I knew in my childhood, where I began giving responses at mass from the age of seven. Outwardly Servandoni's great edifice has nothing in common with the neo-Byzantine building in my village, which dates from the end of the nineteenth century, and has a picturesque onion dome bearing no obvious relationship to the noble architecture of the sixth *arrondissement* in Paris. Although it is ridiculously small compared with Saint-Sulpice, my church nonetheless displays a certain grandeur, even majesty, which is absent from the other churches in the region.

That village church educated me. Saint-Sulpice took over from there, but I still feel the need to return to my lost roots. As an altar boy I not only learned to enjoy the communion wine, I gained some experience about human life. I had a front-row seat for christenings, marriages, and funerals. I held up the salt and the holy oil to the officiating priest, watching the baby's expression as the water was poured on his head and he started to bawl. I closely observed the faces of the prospective man and wife when they pronounced the fatal "I do." I liked making predictions about their future based on the way they spoke and the way they looked. We were obviously mainly interested in the bride. The comments came thick and fast in the sacristy after the ceremony, when we altar boys swapped our impressions: "Did you see that? She looked as if butter wouldn't melt in her mouth!" "Boy, she looks like hot stuff!" We fantasized wildly about the wedding night. In those days there was no trial period. In the country we imagined that the innocent virgin was being taken to the bull. It was either sacrifice or passion. We were very ingenuous. As far as we were concerned there was no middle way: the distasteful aspects of the first experience could not possibly change to delight.

My favorite service by far was the funeral. I loved the somber decorum of the burial service: the tolling of the bell, the cortege all dressed in black, the coffin resting on the catafalque, and the *Dies Irae* that both thrilled and terrified my imagination. Once again I had the best spot when I stood near the coffin and handed the holy water sprinkler to the priest. I experienced the mixed feelings of someone looking into those tearful faces and seeing a suffering he knew nothing about. Always tears and ecstasy. It really was Baudelaire's "religion of universal suffering," but clothed in very earthly splendor.

The mobile crane set up in the Chapel of the Holy Angels has allowed the cameraman to examine every last corner of *Jacob Wrestling with the Angel*. The entrenchment camp Delacroix established here must have looked a little like this installation with its platforms and bridges between. Now it's my turn: I have to reply to the director's questions. Later I'll be able to climb where the cameraman has been and explore the wall. The series is called *The Hidden Man*.[5]

A while ago I asked the cameraman to recount his impressions, and I felt I was questioning him as if he had just climbed Everest. He replied, highly excited:

"It's an incredible sensation. It was like being in the painting. How can I describe it? The wall is a real sculpture. It's built up like a relief. I felt as if I was absorbed into the whole thing."

"Absorbed! Do you mean in the sense of engulfed?"

"Yes. Swallowed up, submerged. You quickly lose your footing in this painting. It's like a relief of a seabed: sand on the bottom, blue silt, red clay... It's deep; there's probably no oxygen," he said, punctuating his words with a forced laugh. "You'll see for yourself when you go up there."

The organ is silent now. Apart from the gleaming recess of the Holy Angels and the red glow from the Chapel of the Virgin, the church is completely plunged in darkness. All signs of life have deserted Saint-Sulpice. There is only the glowing heart beating in Delacroix's chapel. The presence of cables, lights, control panel, not to mention the machinist's gloves, makes one think of an open-heart operation. The Chapel of the Holy Angels is indeed the organ that powers the church, the most important medium in the circulatory system of the building. There are two thumps, then a pause, then two more. These beats are just like the systole and diastole. Where do they come from? Perhaps from air remaining in the organ bellows.

In any event, the artificial light has altered *Wrestling with the Angel*, as if certain parts had been roughed up. It is not obvious, but there is a slight change in orientation, which has mostly disturbed the area around the edges. But the stunning effect of the scene and its solar energy are still there. The darkness of night seems to make the calmness of the angel and his ironic expression all the more apparent. In theory, he is the one who should win the fight. Has the angel, God's messenger, ever been seen to lose? Jacob has already waited for part of the night before their actual confrontation. He knows he is going to face the supreme test. But what will it be? He is alone, like Jesus on the Mount of Olives. He is filled with doubt. He is afraid. "Father, remove this cup from me."

In a few moments his adversary will suddenly appear. The caravan peacefully winds its way through the countryside, paying no attention to the drama being played out, like the apostles who fell asleep. "The spirit is willing but the flesh is weak," Jesus observes. It has been said countless times that Jacob's struggle with the angel was the flesh fighting against the spirit, but it is never actually stated who should win. We know, of course, that the spiritual side should win—or else there is not much hope for the spirit. Everything points to its victory. Then, contrary to all expectation, Jacob wins. It is an eminently ironic situation. Irony reverses things.

"Why do you always talk about the irony of the angel?" the director asks quietly. I scarcely hear his questions. He whispers them. His quick, bright eyes however belie that faraway look he affects, as if I should absolutely forget he is there.

"Well then, what about the irony?"

"The angel seems to be winking at us. Jacob is struggling like mad. The angel is holding him at a distance. As in the theater, when the actor talks to himself but is really addressing the audience, the angel is letting us know quite clearly that he is going to let Jacob win."

"So the fight is fixed?"

"Why? In any match, the favorite can always lose. Those who decide to confront their adversary, even if they have no chance, win in the end: that is the meaning of this fight. Indeed God doesn't like those who are lukewarm; he doesn't much care for those who give up the struggle straight away. It's a glorification of individual responsibility."

"The irony...?"

His is pretty effective. He listens and then comes back to the attack with a word, just one. It's a sharp point that he brandishes as if to burst the bubble of verbosity—that sterile effervescence, which often increases before our eyes and ears the more we speak—and bursts it before we even start.

"It's the vanquished who blesses the victor. That's unheard of."

"And you, you've struggled with the angel."

He caught me on the hop. Besides, it's not a real question. I had a feeling that it was going to come up. He calmly prepared it in his mind, making it sound like a statement of fact.

"With the angel? I'd really have liked that."

A pretty lame way to get out of it. I have always tended to evade this episode in my life. I don't really like people confining me to those three years in detention. I have to keep escaping from the new prison to which they have assigned me. Repetition is the punishment of the ex-hostage. The questions are always the same, and all the former prisoner can do is give the same answer over and over again. The hostage is reduced to one summation and one alone: to be executed. It is his function; he was abducted for that purpose. The hostage is taken to be "taken out" or, if you prefer, to be taken away from the love of his family. (The French language has strange ironies: we literally say *ravished* from the love of his family, and the abductors who make us suffer are called *ravisseurs,* in other words, ravishing people.) And so the questions are inevitably the same. How could it be any different? Only those who have lived through such an ordeal are entitled to ask them, and they are careful not to do so lest they find themselves on show again as they were then.

I try to explain that everyone inevitably has to wrestle with the angel; everyone has his or her own moment of truth! God tests his creatures, in whom he has placed all his goodwill. Like Oedipus, one must fight the sphinx to make him give up his secret. Jacob wrestles with God to gain his blessing, thus acknowledging that He is all-powerful. "No need to spend three years in Beirut for that," I point out to the director. But it is true that the difficult thing is the uncertainty of it: how does one recognize when that struggle should take place? An occasion like that can pass unnoticed. At the time one does not always perceive what is at stake or hear the order given to us to join battle. There are people who will never be aware of the precise moment when their fate irreparably befell them.

"If you look at it from that point of view, I was lucky," I add with a laugh.

"Is that humor or irony?"

"Irony is a form of defense, humor a form of resistance. Humor can cut and run while irony cannot escape. It can only relieve the burden. The supreme irony of the angel is in the reversal of roles: he is blessed by Jacob. But that does not solve anything; it does not mean that he recognizes the future patriarch as all-powerful. If you think about it, this fight is a drawn match. No one has any humor in this story, certainly not Jacob, who takes everything literally. He lowers his head and charges at the stranger without thinking. 'All right then! I'm being attacked, so I'll defend myself,' he seems to be saying. I do like the irony of the angel pretending to be beaten, bringing his opponent around to take stock of himself. It's a forerunner of Socratic irony: the way it works is very educational. Besides, there is something angelic in irony. It's the domain of the in-between, the middle, the unfinished."

"And the struggle takes place in the middle of the ford."

"Yes! The angel has blocked Jacob's path. But what is he refusing him? Delacroix has shown the moment just before the revelation, exactly the moment when the curtain is about to go up. It's very frustrating. We are about to know everything, but we won't actually know anything. Delacroix decided to do it that way, but he said enough about it for us to glimpse what is behind the story."

"Jacob is the story of a disappearance."

"A vanishing, more like it. No one knew where Jacob had gone after he stole his brother's birthright. He had fled. Was he even still alive? This event at Jabbok is the story of a return, but a return that is the supreme test. Everything happens when he reappears. Jacob has made a new life far from his homeland. He has been a success. One day he decides to come back to the land of his birth. He has been released from his Uncle Laban; he is free. But to gain complete freedom, he must confront a possibly fatal scenario. In these moments of truth, man is always alone. Against all odds, he will win the fight he should lose. Divine protection certainly plays a part in it. There is no doubt that his life is spared, he is reborn, but he will never be the same again. Victorious but wounded, he changes his name. As well as that, he is now crippled!"

"Oedipus means 'the lame man.'..."

"Yes, Jacob walks with a limp. Like Talleyrand..."

"Talleyrand?"

"You know what I'm getting at: Delacroix's alleged father, the apostate bishop.... He also had a limp."

"You're getting away from the subject. Anyway you've already told me that it was unlikely he was the father."

Usually so cool and collected, he is now visibly put out. Is it my digression that has disturbed his composure? Or the revelation of a new element in the story?

"It's unlikely, that's a fact. But Delacroix knew the gossip. That he should have made any reference to it, even unconsciously, is another fact. Talleyrand was born a few hundred yards from here in rue Garancière, you know. He was baptized in this church and studied in the Saint-Sulpice seminary. And it was in this very church that he spotted the dancer who became his mistress. But these details no doubt have nothing to do with *Wrestling with the Angel.* As for the limp, I'm not so sure."

"I've noticed that you always create a diversion when things become too personal. Do stop hiding behind Delacroix!"

I don't feel that I have been deluding him. Does he understand that all these threads, stretched and crisscrossed like a loom, had to be set in motion and woven together before I can at last make out the famous central figure in the carpet?

"The central figure is in you," he says with a smile. "But I sense that you're impatient to see the painting. Go on. It's your turn."

In this stark operating-theater lighting, I feel as if I've been undergoing surgery. I wish I had been desensitized before going under the knife.

I have been waiting for this moment for a long time. To be swallowed up into *Jacob Wrestling with the Angel* as the cameraman was...Perhaps I shall never return! Who knows? I am about to sink into the lava of the "Delacroix volcano"—the image comes from Baudelaire.

My heart is beating fast as I climb up the scaffolding. The hat and the clothes in the foreground, which Maurice Denis often made his pupils copy, have little effect on me. And yet that yellow-orange hat has always intrigued me. It is hardly biblical. It looks like something a southern planter would wear. The same hat with the turned-up brim adorns the head of the horseman on the right leading Jacob's flock. I expected to be struck by the famous "*flochetage*" brushstrokes—i.e. short brushstrokes placed side by side or interlaced—on the clothing under the lance. I notice that this Van Gogh crosshatching is more interesting seen from below. On the other hand, I can very clearly see a tear that had revealed the bare plaster behind this still life section. It happened in 1938, at the time of the Munich settlement, when parts of the painting were damaged by sandbags meant to protect it. The scratch was repaired but the restoration still looks like the outline left by a sticking plaster.

And the lance. What does it indicate? I like to think that it is showing a hidden path like the arrow in a cross-country race, but I know it is not so. I have had to yield to the facts for some time now. It is pointing to the angel's crotch, which is a means Delacroix used to emphasize the fact that this person he has chosen to depict is definitely a male. It is obviously very tempting to see the pointed lance as the symbol of triumphant sexuality. In any event, even if Jacob has abandoned his weapon, he has not got rid of his bulky animal skin, the symbol of animal nature and the lower instincts.

Andrieu relates that this still life was done in twenty-two minutes.

The angel's head...I look at the eye, the nose, the blonde hair. It would seem that Delacroix has made the light colors particularly thick. I see nothing but rough surfaces, hatching, and streaks that sometimes look like saber slashes. The whole thing gives the impression of something unfinished. The trunks of the three trees remind me of a host of furrows separated by transverse ridges. This wild fibrillation makes me dizzy. At the same time, the effect of this massive vision of alpine folds is contradicted by an image of blue-green stagnant water, like a lagoon with passages of a murky, almost viscous green. The water looks brackish, muddy in places.

The cameraman was right: this wall is a seabed. More than anything else, I have the strange impression of a painting that has difficulty in becoming part of that wall.

I climb down again straight away. I do not want to sink into the stagnant water that makes me feel so uneasy, almost fearful. I must look like a drowned man, for the director addresses me anxiously: "You've turned quite pale." Delacroix, painting's musician! But one should not look too closely at the chords. Standing next to an instrument, one hears nothing of the real music.

I look warily at the cameraman. What did *he* see? He smiles at me confidently, half knowingly. He didn't speak of drowning; he called it "absorption." I nearly sank like a stone; he said that he had only got out of his depth.

"It's the painting that chooses you...." There is now one more among the elect of *Wrestling with the Angel*.

CHAPTER 13

Removing the Ladder

Angels carrying keys: what locks do they fit? These angels with their rings of keys are on the wall behind *Jacob Wrestling with the Angel*. Perhaps Delacroix looked at the paintings by his neighbor in the next chapel before beginning his own in the Holy Angels.

The Chapel of the Souls in Purgatory, decorated by François-Joseph Heim, was officially opened on 1 October 1842. Delacroix received his commission for the Holy Angels in 1849.

Why did Heim choose to depict angels in his *Prayer for the Dead* on the other side of the wall? It is of course quite natural to see them in a church, but Saint-Sulpice has made them its specialty, both in statuary and painting.

The portrayal of angels is never innocent. It is generally believed that they are there as extras to fill out a religious subject. Wrong! If the angel is the bearer of a message, he is in no way a supernumerary. After Adam's disobedience, God placed cherubim armed with swords to guard the entrance to the Garden of Eden. The angel is the guardian of doors that hide a secret. He is there at the beginning of Genesis and after the disaster. He also closes the Apocalypse, putting the Apostle John firmly in his place when he wants to prostrate himself at his feet.

"Heim, the painter of the *Battle of Rocroy*, had no choice with the paintings that decorate the Purgatory Chapel but to make them tragic. We should nonetheless give him credit for having gone fairly deeply into his difficult subject and created two powerful allegories." This is from an article on "The Paintings of Saint-Sulpice" by Paul Bence.[1] The critic's awkward position is quite apparent here. It is undeniable that Heim "went fairly deeply" into his subject, which was most certainly "difficult." His painting appears as the bad side, the dark, uninviting part of the wall, the section on the opposite side from the light, and not intended to be seen. Besides, building an altar and a base for Clesinger's *Pietà* that would block out the bottom section of the window was a guarantee that it would be hidden.

Allegory, characterized by the personification of abstract ideas, is a tricky, perilous genre. Heim's merit lies in having increased the distress signals. The pick in the foreground tells us that we must dig deep. In addition, there is a ladder in the grave he has chosen to depict. His approach to the subject shows him taking an almost perverse delight in creating problems. Did he want to show that no one could do better and that after him the ladder should be taken away? What is the purpose of the keys the little angel in the upper part is holding? Evidently to open the gates of Heaven. To sum up: there is the ladder, the keys, and that hole. Wouldn't it indicate in Heim the will, or at the very least a wish, to force or open a way through?

The scene is now faded and dull, just a ghost of a painting. The artist's refusal to use color, seeking dark, grey tones instead, explains the dusty look time has given to this wall. Saltpeter has left a chalky film over the surface. Yet in the morning at sunrise, it does happen that the *Prayer for the Dead* comes alive. If the sky is clear an incredible phenomenon can be seen: the muddy colors gain warmth and the bodies spring to life. Even the eye is won over by the harmony and the ingenuity of the painting as a whole. But you have to be quick. Light shines only for a moment in Purgatory.

In that moment a group of people can be clearly seen lamenting at the graveside—the aforementioned grave with the ladder. Who are they mourning? No doubt a beloved relative who will have to languish in the fires of Purgatory, where Death's scythe can clearly be seen. Heavenly creatures bearing keys stand ready to open the gates of Paradise to the just while an angel surveys the scene from above. He looks like a swimmer getting ready to do the backstroke.

Once again the irony is obvious: Heim was given the shadow side of the mountain, the shady side of the wall, the most arid part. Delacroix on the other hand was awarded the sunny south-facing slope, the easy part. It is impossible to believe that during the seven years he worked at Saint-Sulpice, he refused to make a judgment about Heim's work. Contrary to what he thought of the other "daubers" of Saint-Sulpice—the Lafons, the Hesses, or the Signols—he had a good opinion of this artist. Let us not forget that when Delacroix began working in the Chapel of the Holy Angels, he came up against a major technical problem: the preparatory coating of the wall, the same wall that Heim had mastered ten years or so earlier. Delacroix must necessarily have examined his neighbor's work. How did *he* go about it? The creator of *Wrestling with the Angel* must have asked himself that question.

Admittedly he makes no mention of it in the *Journal* or his correspondence. But then he always appears unaware of his surroundings when he is working. And he has always taken care to keep himself to himself, locked away from prying eyes. Self-criticism, if you will, but no confessions! "If ever a man had an ivory tower well defended by bars and locks, it was Eugène Delacroix. Who could be more fond of his ivory tower, that is to say, secrecy?" Baudelaire's tone is quite recognizable in this comment. The painter always refused to give the game away.

The fact that Delacroix does not speak of Heim does not mean that he ignored him. The opposite is probably true. There are obvious correspondences between the two paintings. They answer each other and send energy through the thickness of the wall. You will not be surprised to learn that Delacroix is the positive pole. The negative represented by Heim is in no way derogatory. The forces of attraction and repulsion acting on this wall are the same and absolutely interdependent, even though the electric brightness is only visible on one side. It is as if *Jacob Wrestling with the Angel* needed to be charged, drawing energy from the *Prayer for the Dead.*

When he saw Heim's painting, Delacroix had no need to use it as a counterexample—he had too much confidence in his own talent—but the allegory was there as a model to be reversed. Delacroix, who spent a lot of his time copying the masterpieces of the past to learn their secrets, never turned his back on what his contemporaries could teach him, if only to benefit from their mistakes. He was the incarnation of modernity but had absolutely no faith in it. He thought that new ideas do not create men of genius. The only thing that counted was "the idea that possesses them; that what has been said has still not been said enough." Repeat, but say it better.

Many details in the Chapel of the Holy Angels refer to Heim. No doubt the splendor of *Wrestling with the Angel* refers back to the sepulchral *Prayer for the Dead.* No doubt the dawn of the world just arising under the colossal trees is a match with the fading twilight of Purgatory. But most important of all, that ladder in the grave is a clear allusion to Jacob's dream, which, for that matter, is just as enigmatic as the crossing of the Jabbok ford. What does Jacob see in this dream? "A ladder set up on the earth" and "the angels of God ascending and descending on it." These details are the framework of Jacob's dream. In Heim's painting they convey a feeling of distress. Jacob expresses it when he says: "How dreadful is this place." And the biblical narrator adds: "This is none other than the house of God, and this is the gate of heaven," also a feature in Heim's painting with the angels holding rings of keys. Biblical commentators have not failed to point out the similarities between Jacob's dream and his fight with the angel: both take place at night and bring fear, with the father figure clearly a presence.

Is there complicity, connivance, or correspondence between these paintings? Perhaps. Fusion? Certainly not. There is one material fact that cannot be got round: these two paintings, separated by a yard of thickness, cover the same wall. Delacroix's initial preparations, which were absorbed too quickly, must have penetrated very close to the coating Heim had put on his side. Let us call it twinning, fraternal twins, nonidentical twins.

Moreover, an injustice still persists here. No one looks at Heim. All they want to see is Delacroix. Some signs are unmistakable. You can see in photos taken at the beginning of the twentieth century that there was a confessional in the Chapel of the Holy Angels. Confession is still the specialty of the priests at Saint-Sulpice (sixty to eighty a day). This confessional had been placed below *Wrestling with the Angel* and encroached on the bottom part of the painting. It was moved. Where was it stored? In the next chapel, the Souls in Purgatory. The place looks more and more like a storeroom. "Kindly do not put anything down on this altar," a notice requests. And where did they put this confessional? Below the *Prayer for the Dead*, of course.

*   *   *

François-Joseph Heim is fascinating because he has not left behind any real information about himself. He is not unknown to those who are interested in nineteenth-century painting, but outside of specialists in the field, who knows his name today? There is no trace of him, apart from his painting. Heim was born in Belfort in 1787 and died in Paris in 1865, but he does not seem to have a biography. A few dictionaries do, however, note several facts—always the same ones.

Joining Vincent's studio in 1803, he was a fellow student of Horace Vernet. He won second place in the 1806 Prix de Rome and spent several years at the Villa Medici. His first success came in 1812. Guess who is the central figure in this work: Jacob. Is that by chance? It does not portray *Jacob Wrestling with the Angel*, but it is not far from it. The event has a connection with crossing the Jabbok ford. Jacob, who has tricked his sightless father and stolen his father's blessing from his brother Esau, has to flee the land of Canaan and take refuge with his Uncle Laban. The work is entitled *The Arrival of Jacob in Mesopotamia*.

I may be going down a blind alley, but I secretly hope that this picture, which I finally discovered is in the Bordeaux Musée des Beaux-Arts, will help me to understand Delacroix's painting. The character of Jacob must have fascinated Heim as he submitted *Joseph's Coat Brought Back to Jacob* to the Salon of 1817. This event in Jacob's life takes place long after the night at Jabbok, during the patriarch's last years. Joseph's brothers are jealous and devise a plan to get rid of him. They sell him to merchants and take home Joseph's coat of many colors, which they have dipped in goat's blood, telling their father Jacob that his favorite son was killed by a wild beast.

Fame comes to Heim with *Charles X Rewarding Artists*, shown at the Salon of 1824. It is the classic career of an artist whose inclination was to treat historical and religious subjects in vogue during the Restoration. He is considered to be the Bourbons' appointed artist. Although commissions do not cease during the July Monarchy, he already seems old-fashioned. He is criticized for his academicism. The only known occurrence that gives him a flesh-and-blood existence takes place in 1831. While he is working on one of the ceilings in the Louvre, he has a fall, which keeps him out of action for a long time. Heim then seems to go back to his outdated notions. He is considered a painter past his time.

That is an unfair assessment. I came across one of his pictures painted in 1840 in the municipal gallery at Semur-en-Auxois. It is called *The Prisoner*. It shows a naked man lying on the ground. The drawing is superb, and the pose, although frozen, conveys the anguish of silent suffering. The strangeness of the scene, the hyper-realistic detail of the body, and the very Caravaggesque sense of light and setting cannot fail to make the viewer curious. Who was this prisoner? What was Heim wanting to depict? The painter never gave any details.

The Second Empire resurrects Heim's popularity. Appointed as president of the Académie des Beaux-Arts in 1853, he has a great triumph at the World Exhibition of 1855 with *The Victories of Judas Maccabaeus* and *The Battle of Rocroy*. In 1859 he exhibits a series of pencil portraits of the members of the institute (he must therefore have drawn Delacroix, a member of the Académie des Beaux-Arts for the last two years!) Praises are heaped on him, notably by Baudelaire who admires his sketches for showing "a marvelous understanding of the way humans pull faces." Heim's drawings are indeed astonishing. They have a sense of detail and an ease of execution combined with psychological insight. They are so different from his sometimes stiff and formal paintings.

All these facts give some idea of the work but tell us little about the personality of the man. Who was Heim? In what circles did he move? I wrote to the museum in his birthplace, Belfort, which has several of his paintings, to try and find some information. No result. Heim died relatively unnoticed in 1865. How many members of parliament would know that he decorated the Palais Bourbon and the Hôtel de Lassay?

Then I was lucky enough to come across an article by the curator of paintings in the Louvre, Jean-Pierre Cuzin.[2] Although this paper is still the best overview of Heim's work, we would nevertheless like to know more about the man. Cuzin says in conclusion, "This paper is only an outline, and an appeal to a young art historian to undertake, and quickly, a complete study of an artist who deserves it." He also says of Heim that he is "perhaps the last representative in France of what could be called traditional painting and, as such, somewhat out of place in the middle of the nineteenth century."

The words he uses to describe *Jacob in Mesopotamia* arouse my curiosity: "It makes an impression with the strength of the semisculptural treatment of space and the starkness of the lighting." The article contains a black-and-white reproduction of the painting. Jacob is wearing a delightful little hat. However, a part of the picture is completely blackened. As often happens with Heim, the strangeness of his paintings comes from their stillness and precision: both people and landscape seem rooted to the spot.

An atmosphere of unreality seems to float in the air, emphasized by the stark contrast between the dark background and the way Jacob is standing.

CHAPTER 14

"I think it will be the death of me"

The sacristan of Saint-Sulpice opens the door that I have been so curious about. Delacroix used this opening, leading toward the Peristyle Chapel, in the composition of *Heliodorus*. In the painting, the doorway leads down to the foreground and is the pivotal point of the scene. Delacroix has spread the treasures of the Temple around the lintel. He carefully wrote his name there among the gold and jewels: DELACROIX, 1861. In capital letters and Didot font. No Eugène.

I am all the keener to see the Peristyle Chapel since I learned that the Dauphin's organ had been stored there. Being of no further use after the restoration of the great organ, this instrument has been moved many times. In 1926 it was decided to put it behind *Heliodorus*. I have not been able to find out who made this decision.

The Dauphin's organ, which was in the Petit Trianon at Versailles when the Revolution broke out, was sold at auction by two commissioners of the Republic. One of these two representatives was none other than Charles Delacroix. His son Eugène knew of this instrument since it was in the Chapel of the Virgin, in full view of all, at the time when he was working on *Wrestling with the Angel*.

Did the person who decided to move the organ in 1926 and store it behind *Heliodorus* have a sense of humor or irony? I would incline toward irony, especially as there is a *Death of Saint*

Joseph hidden under an arch at the back of *Heliodorus*. The chapel was actually dedicated for some time to Jesus's "foster father." The backing of a foster father...The allusion to Charles Delacroix is, of course, purely involuntary. But how many strange things crop up in this story! All these competing elements: a real combination of circumstances.

Long closed to the public, the chapel is a real treasure in itself. Even though it is hidden inside the church, one can hear all the sounds of the city, but muted by the height of the vault. The Louis XVI rotunda has eight Corinthian columns. The floor, richly paved with a marble rose pattern, is further enhanced with an extraordinary motif extending the perspective effect produced by the cupola. The ceiling is not entirely closed over. It was originally designed to accommodate a stairwell giving access to the library, which was to be on the first floor behind the loggia. This huge Roman-style balcony, reminiscent of papal blessings, can be seen from the square. Another of Servandoni's ideas.

We are now behind *Heliodorus*. The sacristan has brought a powerful flashlight and a pair of binoculars with him. He hands them to me and asks me to look carefully at one of the medallions on top of a statue of Hope. It explains a detail: the Tablets of the Law held by the little angels. I can make out the engraved words: RIGHTS OF MAN AND CITIZEN.

The Dauphin's organ is no longer there; it has returned to Versailles, its former home. But at least there is still that reminder of the revolutionary period when "the temple of Saint-Sulpice" was dedicated to the Supreme Being, and later to the creed of theophilanthropy.

There is one painting decorating the Peristyle Chapel: *Noli me tangere*, do not touch me. A bloodstained Christ keeps a tearful

Mary Magdalene at arm's length. The picture blocks a window, which used to look out on to the rue Palatine.

On an earlier occasion I had already discovered under this chapel a place that left a strange impression on my mind. It was on a summer afternoon. The sacristan and I were in a narrow underground passageway beneath the church, which was beautifully built with white stone. We suddenly came upon an enormous tiled well, a kind of huge funnel that still had some of the original scaffolding around it. "The oubliettes[1] of Saint-Sulpice," the sacristan said as a joke. This place, the most remote spot in the church, smelled of old fur and looked like an inaccessible circular cell.

We had to hammer open the door of this dungeon. I'm told that it is situated underneath the Peristyle Chapel and the Holy Angels. Yet another prison under Delacroix's wall.

When you approach the Peristyle Chapel, it seems to give a warning. Generally speaking, there is no admittance to it. Although the door has been shut up for a long time, it leads directly to the forecourt. Actually, the chapel is just playing dead. Furthermore, in the nineteenth century it was called the Chapel of the Good Death.

When Delacroix began work in the Holy Angels, the church council built a passage under the scaffolding in order to give access to the Peristyle Chapel. Let us try to imagine this unlikely passage underneath the planks, while on the heights the master wrestled with (or was it against?) the wall. Did he really feel he needed to be so secluded? While the works were going on, the Chapel of the Holy Angels naturally aroused some curiosity. Théophile Gautier, an admirer of the painter, was bursting with impatience as he waited for the moment when the chapel would finally be "unmasked." He speaks of that "mysterious fence of planks that has so often frustrated our desire to enter."

Théophile Gautier's impatience is understandable, for at the end of 1857 Delacroix is still far from finished. It is in fact the least productive year in the Holy Angels. On 28 December he moves his lodgings from rue Notre Dame de Lorette to number 6 rue Furstenberg to be nearer to Saint-Sulpice. The year 1858 begins and work still has not started again. In July he leaves Paris for Plombières. His *Journal* gives the impression of a man more and more preoccupied with his health and that "wretched digestion." Food lies heavy in his stomach and makes his life a misery. He thinks he has found an explanation for it in Balzac's novel, *Les Paysans*. He copies out a passage on the results of too much tobacco, coffee, and brandy, underlining this sentence: "All excessive consumption affecting the mucous membranes will shorten life." Delacroix happens to see the Emperor who is also taking the waters. "He met me by chance and did me the honor of inquiring after my health," he writes with a certain pride to his cousin Berryer.

He goes back to Paris in September. "I am back to work at Saint-Sulpice. I spend a lot of time on *Heliodorus*. Then the next day, I cannot do a thing...." Is it the urgency or the importance of the project that gives him such a block? No doubt he is sick, but the awareness that he is not finishing makes him feel even worse. He is doggedly persistent, as if his life depended on it. He has a certain masochistic tendency to confuse physical weakness with difficulty in finishing a task. This ambiguity could suggest sexual incompetence—from his youth he has been obsessed with the fiasco of failure to perform.

Some newspapers announce that he has finished the Chapel of the Holy Angels. He is furious. "I ask you, what rogues journalists are." All the same, this false report seems to have given him a new burst of energy. "I have been sweating away at my great work in Saint-Sulpice for three weeks," he writes to his cousin Lamey. He adds, "I have put in a real effort, which I hope will allow me to finish next year." But winter comes, making him interrupt his work once again. He does not like to paint in the cold and dreads the lack of light.

He starts again in the spring. He is satisfied with the work already accomplished. On 27 June 1859, the administration pays him "an installment of five thousand francs," proof that the paintings are well advanced. But in August, Delacroix once again feels the irresistible urge to visit his relatives in the provinces. It is a need he has felt during the whole time he has spent working at Saint-Sulpice. It often coincides with times of doubt or of suffering Delacroix chooses not to mention.

The second part of the *Journal* seems to have lost the spontaneity and sincerity of the earlier writing. Self-censorship is often in evidence after 1847. Having become something of a celebrity, he watches what he says and does for self-protection. He suspects that these notes may be published one day, whereas the youthful trials and hopes he recorded earlier were unpremeditated and for himself alone.

A painful year for Delacroix is 1859. The eight paintings he submits to the Salon should have been the crowning glory of his career, completing the triumph he had in 1855. Among the eight canvases he has chosen is *The Ascent to Calvary*, a subject he had thought of for the transept of Saint-Sulpice, well before the Chapel of the Holy Angels. The painter's choice gets a bad reaction, which shows that at that time the creator of *Sardanapalus* was far from being the established artist that his official commissions or entry to the institute might lead us to believe. Maxime Du Camp—the friend of Flaubert's youth—asked the same question: "Can death have struck Monsieur Eugène Delacroix? I mean the intimations of death that paralyze the hand, close the eyes, and wipe the idea of what is right and true from the mind."

Odilon Redon, who will also paint a *Jacob Wrestling with the Angel*, is eighteen at that time. He describes a strange scene that took place after a reception at the Préfecture. Overcome with admiration, he cannot bring himself to approach the master, so decides to follow him. "He crossed Paris in the darkness, walking like a cat on the narrowest footpaths, head down, deep in thought. A notice with the word *pictures* caught his attention. He went up to it, read it, then set off again preoccupied with his dream, or rather his obsession."

On that night Delacroix absentmindedly went to rue Notre Dame de Lorette, where he had not lived for two years. Realizing his mistake, he calmly made his way back to rue Furstenberg. An odd story, showing that the old artist, lost in his own world, must have paid little attention to his surroundings. However, the word *pictures* was enough to make him alert again. What was he thinking at that moment in front of the paint shop? I wonder what fantasy was going around the head of this man who was so good at giving substance to dreams.

In reality, he slipped his moorings some time ago. He no longer lives among men. His spirit has never weakened; the body is the problem. In a letter dated September 1859, he states: "I have thrown myself into my work, which is progressing well. I am perhaps being overconfident, but I think the results will be good." Contrary to what he has always done in the past, he decides to work in the winter. As a result, Baltard, the chief architect of the City of Paris, states that Delacroix's work "is three quarters done."

One might imagine that the task is almost finished, but the last quarter will prove to be the most taxing part of all. His health deteriorates. He toils more and more over his work and has to take to his bed in January 1860. Boulangé, who is helping him at Saint-Sulpice, is not making progress. On 7 April Delacroix makes a surprise appearance in the chapel. "Boulangé was not expecting me. This infamous rogue does not come, does not work."

For Delacroix, 1860 is a terrible year. He gives the impression of being a man whose health is failing and who is dragging himself about. "I have only been able to work for about a week and then I felt exhausted again," he writes on 23 August. Once again he has to go and rest at Champrosay.

He seems to feel better in September. Every morning at 5:30 he goes to the station at Ris to catch the train, works for three or four hours at Saint-Sulpice, and comes back to Champrosay early to enjoy the countryside. He goes to bed at 8:00 P.M. It's a dog's life. There is only one thing that Delacroix really fears: getting a cold. On 11 November he catches a chill. As for being a cold, it is more the cancer of the larynx, which is getting worse. Even though he is exhausted, Delacroix nevertheless tries to keep his spirits up. "If my health does not fail me, I hope to finish at the beginning of January." He likes to go to his chapel in Saint-Sulpice. "Its appeal is so strong that I rush there, as a healthy young man rushes to meet his mistress."

Healthy? He would like to think so, as if he were still twenty and in love. "To tell the truth, painting harasses and torments me in a thousand ways, like the most demanding mistress. For four months I am off at dawn, rushing to this captivating work, as if to the most beloved mistress."

Such enthusiasm has a hollow ring to it. The comments he makes to his cousin Berryer at this time contradict this eagerness. "Finishing requires a heart of steel: I have to make decisions about everything, and there are difficulties where I never expected to find them." Then he adds this sentence: "I think it will be the death of me."

He knows now that his time is limited. His state of health deteriorates. He is tormented by the thought of not finishing the work. Energy is not what is lacking in this sick body—stoicism is a virtue he both admires and practices—but the poor old frame finds it harder and harder to support this superhuman effort. The months of February, March, and April see Delacroix in a merciless struggle with his wall. It is the painter's last achievement. The will to finish and his exceptional stubbornness have not only got the better of the chapel, but also of his illness, which goes into a remission.

There is something ecstatic in these last brushstrokes. On his platform in the Holy Angels, Delacroix is literally transported, drawn out of himself. He is focussed and wholly concentrated on the very wellspring of his painting. He is absolutely at one with *Wrestling with the Angel* and is just about to complete it. It is as though he is levitating, like Heim's angel on the other side of the wall.

In this ending, which strangely foreshadows his own death, one can feel him overflowing with an invisible energy. This intangible, almost supernatural presence can be compared with the words he utters a few days before he dies: "Oh! If I get better, as I hope to, I will do amazing things. I can feel my brain seething with ideas!"

It is *rapture*. Delacroix is enthralled. But never in the final ecstasy was the body such a presence. He finished his painting by sheer strength, by the power in his wrist. This joint supporting the hand is all-important. "The wrist alone, and not the hand, makes the brush move. The hand only holds the tool that writes, draws or paints; it remains, so to speak, severely stiff, and does nothing more than follow the movement of the wrist."

The body, which he sometimes scathingly called "this worthless thing," is now nothing more than a material object required to obey orders. Delacroix will continue to bear the stigmata in his flesh, as Jacob did. And they will be fatal. It is the price that has to be paid, the last trial before illumination. He has gone through bad patches, times when he could do nothing at all, the artist's dark night. Now the final blazing light.

On 22 July 1861, Delacroix finished the Chapel of the Holy Angels. He had only two more years to live.

CHAPTER 15

The Kestrel Hovering in the Air

It's a scorching day in July 1999 and I have lost my way once again behind the scenes in Saint-Sulpice, even though the sacristan gave me directions from the bottom of the stairs. I have to go to an artist's studio in a kind of attic above the Chapel of the Virgin. The spiral staircase, which goes up several floors, is in the shape of a perfect oval. It's the work of Daniel Gittard, the other great architect of Saint-Sulpice with Servandoni. A man of the classical era and contemporary of Louis XIV, Gittard was the first to think of making this church theatrical. The Corinthian pillars framing the great arcades in the choir and nave are his idea. He planned all that part like a theater. Servandoni's work at the entrance simply follows the spirit of the original architect.

The hot summer weather intensifies the smell of dry dust, an odor of old mildewed material stiffened by the heat wave. The top steps of the staircase are propped up by metal posts, a reminder of the generally dilapidated state of the church.

To get to the studio occupied by the sculptor I am to meet, I have to go across the galleries in the ambulatory, where restoration is in progress. I pass several workmen stripped to the waist. They walk around in these heights with their trowels and plastering tools, and don't seem at all surprised when I appear. Perhaps they have already seen me on previous occasions when I have been exploring.

The white stone of the church looks dazzling in the July sunlight. There does not seem anything modern about this world of winches, pulleys, ladders, and ropes, which hark back to the time the church was built. The minimal clothing of the workmen could be the same worn by journeymen in the Ancien Régime. One of them, dressed in blue twill trousers, has a back covered in tattoos. In answer to my question, he points out a staircase giving access to other rooms under the roof.

I reach a passage. Broken chairs and chipped water pitchers of the type that used to be seen on landings lie on the floor. I open doors to empty rooms. There are dismantled sinks, broken shelves, rickety tables, old-fashioned water-heaters: a vision more of neglect than desolation. There is a smell of old plaster and grease in the air. These passages, antechambers and poky little rooms, must have still been in use in the 1960s. The inner depths of Saint-Sulpice must have been humming with life like the interior of a large building. A whole population of vergers, sacristans, bell-ringers, people who worked the organ bellows, with their cats, hot water bottles, and wallpaper lived in the countless lodgings available behind the scenes. This part, which the public never saw, was the most lively of all. In 1924 it was decided to fit out two little lodgings above the Chapel of Saint John the Baptist. Doors had to be forced open that had been closed since 1793.

Now that men have dispensed with their gods and the invisible world no longer holds sway, the number of people employed by the church has slowly been reduced in line with the disappearance of the faithful.

The door has a notice stating "No Admittance." What a lot of doors in Saint-Sulpice with no admittance! The wind blows through the gap. Where does this nasty smell of stuffy attic and filthy clothes come from? The dismal sound of papers blown by gusts of wind rustles across the floor. I would love to force my way through that forbidden door! I am fascinated by a tiny piece of cardboard pinned to the door. The edges are torn, and it is scarcely bigger that the rusty head of the drawing pin. There must have been a name, a visiting card on the door no longer used today. The recent history of Saint-Sulpice is all about sealed-up passages. The territory had become too big to maintain, so its size had to be reduced. As with a ship taking water, compartments had to be isolated and bulkheads made watertight to save the hull. A chain around the door handles makes it look even more abject. A padlock dangles from it.

I stand in front of the door with no admittance, and knock. No one there. The silence seems to flow toward me from inside the forbidden room, oozing out slowly as from an infected wound. It is broken only by the occasional crackling of dried leaves.

I am definitely lost. I decide to return to the white gallery where the men are working, but I can't manage to find my way back in this maze. I suddenly get a strong whiff of the henhouse, that acrid, sweetish smell of birds' feathers.

I notice an opening in an attic room. A pale light spreads out from it. It is an oculus, one of the many round windows in the walls of the church that give it this remarkable light. This bull's-eye window with its colored glass is particularly interesting because it is set so high up in the wall. It opens on to one of the chapels on the south side and does not let in any light from outside. The gold-painted glass panels are in a bad state, the frame and mounting of the lead strips have come apart. The oculus can be partly opened like a window. I pull the hook.

Almost as though I had broken into the building, the interior of Saint-Sulpice suddenly appears beneath my feet. A mystery box, a box for precious rings, dark as a cedar casket. No one can see me. The visitors down below look microscopic. But the most surprising thing is the dull silver shimmer, which makes the church look all the more barren. Rodin, who wrote about Saint-Sulpice, is right when he says that, as in a landscape, "what is beautiful in architecture is the air." Space, enormously expanded by the high windows, is what links everything in the church. Instead of creating a void, it brings the immense interior to life. When the aquarium light comes in contact with the grey color of the walls, it emulsifies the atmosphere, especially above the choir bathed in a pearly glow.

The gods have withdrawn, but, like other French or European churches, Saint-Sulpice refuses to accept this fate. Anne of Austria laid the first stone in 1646, and the old building is defending itself inch by inch. The Divine Body is still there, but it is obvious that men no longer wish to enter into that communion.

I can see the tabernacle lamp from the oculus, where I can look down on the nave and the choir. Such a tiny, insubstantial presence, which accentuates the absence and deprivation; such a fragile presence in the wilderness of the world. Yet the flame resists and persists. For how long? It is not sadness that I feel looking down on the great body of this church, deserted but still sensual; it is more an intimation of disaster.

From my seat in the gods, I gaze down at the immense theater at my feet, so huge that it seems abandoned, as if after a farewell party. I feel suddenly overwhelmed, perhaps because of this cocoonlike silence. It is too soothing. The solitude scares me.

After being expelled from the Garden of Eden, man finds himself naked for the second time. He has lost a little more of his innocence. The sickness that afflicts Saint-Sulpice highlights this fragile existence more than ever. How can the building be protected, preserved, and consolidated? But above all, what would replace it if a decision is made not to save it? Statues, pulpits, screens, stained-glass windows, and paintings are orphans now, cut off from the fervor of their people. A wedding or a funeral revives a vague sentimentality, but the break with their origins seems irreparable. The long procession of prophets, pietas, and Christs in majesty are still alive, but that life is diminishing. The defense of the national heritage has granted it a reprieve, but the mainspring is broken. The energizing cause that gave these images a soul has died. The faith and adoration of the faithful are no longer there to keep it vibrant.

Muffled movements down below have just broken the silence of the church's lethargic atmosphere. It is a group of tourists. Tiny specks are moving around the astronomical dial—not strictly speaking a work of art. Almost invisible from where I am standing, the visitors are examining the instrument with its copper rod set into the stone floor. Today the meridian is nothing more than a scientific curiosity, a museum piece, but in those days it was used to calculate Easter precisely, those moveable feasts that used to define our ancestors' cosmology. A rule of life has gone. That art that sang of the glory of God and His saints with such enchantment is now *disenchanted*, to quote Marcel Gauchet.[1]

From my bull's-eye window I look down on the deserted chapels. A deathly silence has surrounded their altars since mass stopped being celebrated there. These chapels are no longer incarnate. The flesh of the believers, representing the Divine Body, is dead and gone. The chapels are empty niches; only the main altar is still alive.

The church is more and more like an old ship heading into the wind with its distress lamp at the prow. The noises from the nave are dull, but they still reach me with surprising intensity. They flow like sonar waves and are quite separate from the hubbub of the town. The steps of the visitors in the church sound muted yet fluid, like gently dripping water. A smell of wax and mold rises up from the nave.

Many cathedrals, like Chartres, have their labyrinth in a design on the floor. The meanders represent the path taken by Jesus from the time of his arrest to Calvary. The faithful follow it on their knees. It seems that the maze symbolizes a cabalistic tradition dating from the time of King Solomon. In the case of Saint-Sulpice, the labyrinth is to be found under the roofs. After groping my way through an interlacing pattern of passages, dusty garrets, and poky little holes, I finally find the staircase again. The tattooed workman is breaking plaster. He stifles a smile as he sees me reappear. I explain to him that I lost my way. He thinks he knows where the studio is and offers to take me there.

We find ourselves outside, working our way through a forest of obelisks, buttresses, and domes, stepping over roof gutters, roofing, pipes, and joists. The lead, copper, and slate sparkle in the sunlight. In the intense summer heat, the stone bakes, turns golden, and develops streaks and spots in various shades of saffron. Even the bluish grey of the lead sheets lights up. On the elliptical roof of the Chapel of the Virgin, the five-pointed copper star is lightning bright in the sunshine.

Lower down, a stone statue of a pelican feeding its young with its own flesh stands on top of the Chapel of the Assumption. It looks mortally wounded. The pelican, symbol of paternal love...

The various sets of scaffolding, pushed close against the wall of the building, are enveloped in awning that flaps and tears in the wind. They look like the mobile towers of some barbarian camp. The more tightly they are attached to their prey, the more easily they can seize it.

This is the aerial world of Saint-Sulpice, soaring above the town, spreading a warm smell of sourdough into the atmosphere. The kestrel hovers in the air near the south tower where he has made his home. On this early summer day, everything seems to hang in the sharp, burning air.

The falcon suddenly dives down into the covered balcony toward the statue of Saint Sulpice. I don't see it fly up again. Feathers float gently in the blinding light.

The tattooed workman points to a two-story apartment set into one of the terraces. A house in the air! There are flowers blooming at the windows, cretonne curtains filtering the light. The scrolled ironwork is magnificently chased. This charming house is hidden out of sight behind an archway. A red-headed man comes out and pensively says good day. "He lives there. He's very discreet. He does his best to pass unnoticed," my companion informs me. That is probably the best way to attract attention! Is he the man the sacristan told me about?

We go into a part of the labyrinth that had disorientated me. Little bushes flourish on the crumbling cornices. The worn stone dissolves and loses its sharp edges like a damp sugar cube. The workman stops in front of a door with the notice CHAPEL OF THE HOLY ANGELS above it.

"There it is," he says.

"I'm not looking for the attic above the Chapel of the Holy Angels," I reply, rather peeved.

"Who told you that? You are looking for the sculptress's studio. I think it's here. You only have to knock. Good luck!" he says softly before moving off.

The words written on the notice in the style of Latin inscriptions with triangular impasto are typically nineteenth century. This is obviously not its original location.

The door opens. A tall, graceful, elderly lady appears in the doorway. "Ah! There you are! I was afraid you might have lost your way." The direct, rather stern manner with which she looks at me is calm and self-possessed. I have an impression of fragility and determination. "I know of some who have never found their way back. They're still wandering about in there. Don't you hear them moaning?" she asks playfully. We strain our ears. And indeed I can hear the wind, sometimes murmuring, sometimes shrill.

"You do hear them, don't you?" she declares, laughing out loud.

"The moans don't prove anything. All churches complain: they all moan and groan."

"This one has something to complain about. It's suffering. It needs to be taken care of. Have you seen the work they're doing? They're coming closer. One day I'll have to leave."

She speaks with an American accent, which is not surprising as she was born in Buffalo in New York State.

"The notice! I can see that it intrigues you. Would you believe it? I found it among the rubble. It should probably be hung in the attic space above the Chapel of the Holy Angels. Do come in!"

There are angels everywhere, set in serried ranks on the mantelpiece, the tables, shelves, and stools. The celestial horde has taken over the studio. There is a poster pinned to the wall showing an army of archangels lined up as if on parade. She tells me that it is *The Heavenly Army* by Rudolfo Guariento in the Padua Gallery. Some of the angels she has sculpted have flames on their heads like certain paintings by Fra Angelico.

"They're not related to those," she points out, sounding a little surly. "Neither are the wings. Everything is carved from the block."

"Why do you carve only angels?"

"I have a particular devotion to them," she explains, and her voice grows gentler. "To me they're living beings. They're close to me. I have a wonderful time with them."

Then she adds rather curtly, as if I thought she was a fanatic, "But of course I can't see them."

One senses that she has a radiant inner life, a great experience of contemplation, which should not be mistaken, she seems to imply, for some sort of mysticism.

The studio is very charming. It used to be an apartment with moldings, ceiling ornamentation, and flooring that come from the Louis XV period. My hostess tells me that the rooms were once a priest's living quarters. The studio in the old drawing room is furnished with a little sofa, a low table, Thonet chairs, and a bookshelf. The superb floor is antique oak parquetry laid at right angles.

"This is a gift from heaven," she exclaims. "There are leaks into the studio sometimes, as there are all over this church, but it's a privilege to work on the rooftops in the heart of Paris."

Then she adds, speaking more softly with an almost painful emotion in her voice,

"My days are numbered here, but no one knows when it will happen. I shall have to leave with my angels," she says with a sigh.

"Angels seem to be Saint-Sulpice's specialty."

"Yes, but I was already sculpting angels before I came here."

"I was mainly thinking of Delacroix."

"Our whole life on earth is a struggle with the angel. Although it's often said, I don't think that the angel in Delacroix's painting represents God. One doesn't wrestle with God," she says almost sharply.

"Was that of any concern to Delacroix? He was an agnostic!"

"Wasn't he the one who said, 'God is within us'? What more is there to say?"

"Nothing, I agree. But that doesn't prevent us from wondering why he chose the theme of wrestling with the angel."

"Yes, it's strange. Do you know that while he was working in the Holy Angels, he relaxed by painting *Lion Hunts*, bloodthirsty tigers, nothing but cruel subjects!"

A muffled booming can be clearly heard in the walls. They sound vaguely metallic, like hammering on the hull of a ship in dry dock. I pause for a moment before proceeding.

"I'm convinced most of all that Delacroix had no illusions about mankind. To him human beings were nothing more than bestial creatures wholly driven by the will to dominate. 'A common feeling motivates man,' he wrote one day in his *Journal*, 'to get ahead at all costs, trampling over his neighbor's body on the way.'"

"Yes, but all the same his paintings prove that he believed in man's divine side."

"In the angel within him?"

"Yes. Besides, it's not the only side that interests me," she says.

She makes a sweeping gesture with her hand, indicating the celestial host inhabiting the studio.

A much louder banging resounds like gunfire, making the whole room shake. It reverberates in the air like a muffled explosion.

"As I was saying to you, it's coming closer! It's all very upsetting. The thought of moving. Where would I go? The work benches, the tools, all take up a lot of room. Sculpture is a cumbersome art," she sighs.

During later explorations of the building, I have often come back and knocked on her studio door. No one has appeared. Perhaps she didn't want to meet me again. Or had she been forced to leave as she feared?

Every day from the rue Palatine I see the mobile towers moving closer to her studio high in the air. The netting on the scaffolding flaps in the wind like birds' wings.

Have the angels been evicted?

CHAPTER 16

The Sacred Tetragrammaton

Never seek an immediate result; prowl around far from your objective and you will have a much better chance of zeroing in on it. These principles have been very helpful until now, although after a promising start I have also sometimes reached a complete halt.

For example, I remember coming across a novel called *The Nights of Lutetia* in 1993.[1] A large part of the story takes place in the Chapel of the Holy Angels. It is the place where the hero has his romantic rendezvous. Ever since Casanova and the Chevalier des Grieux, who found Manon Lescaut again in Saint-Sulpice, libertines have often met their prey in churches. The sacrilegious aspect arouses them. Admittedly it is the house of God but as he is a God of love, he should probably find nothing wrong with that. (During the grim Fascist years between the wars, the chapel was also the favorite meeting place of the Italian Leftists.) Besides, there is nothing licentious in *The Nights of Lutetia*. The author, David Shahar, who is an Israeli, gives a long description of *Wrestling with the Angel*. Like all those who have been captivated by this painting, he is convinced that it contains a hidden purpose. Paradoxically, the heroine named Lutèce says that she hates the church and "its dramatic display of Christian virtue." The church gives her a feeling of awful oppression. She does not like Delacroix either, judging him too theatrical and high flown.

I like the way this novel confuses the issue, subtly manipulating false assumptions and missed opportunities to deceive the reader. "Should one trust appearances?" asks David Shahar, who sums up the question in these words: "Is there any connection between the way people look and the way they really are?"

I got it into my head that this writer was looking for the same thing I was. He lived in Jerusalem, so I wrote to him care of his publisher. No reply. Time went by. One day at the Extraordinary Travelers Festival in Saint Malo, I found myself engaged in a debate on a subject I have since forgotten. I can remember only some verbal sparring with a man I took to be a Breton. His fisherman's cap, the deeply etched lines on his face, his bluff but cordial directness, all indicated a native of Brittany. But my fisherman was none other than David Shahar, the man I had been trying to contact.

We went and had a few drinks in the town bars, and he told me the story of *The Nights of Lutetia*. Everything started with the north tower of Saint-Sulpice.

"I didn't know this church. When I first saw it, I felt intimidated by its massive size. Then I noticed an intriguing inscription in Hebrew. It was engraved on the triangular pediments near the top of the tall tower. It was the sacred tetragrammaton of the divine name YHWH! A Jew is forbidden to say it. It's the unutterable name. What was this Hebrew inscription doing in a Christian church? I went inside. The first thing I saw was *Jacob Wrestling with the Angel*. This symbolizes a major event in the history of my people. The birth of Israel! I wrote in my book that Delacroix made a mistake. He painted an angel instead of a man. He has no determinate sex. This uncertainty is very strange. In my opinion the angel is terrified. Jacob has hit him below the belt. The heroine in my book exclaims: 'God is afraid!'"

I was very struck by this observation, and told him that I found it puzzling. "I don't understand. Is it God, an angel, or a man?" He replied that the account in Genesis, made up of several superimposed versions, had been revised at different times to make it conform to Jewish orthodoxy. "One doesn't fight with God. The text carefully avoids naming him. That's why he later had to be transformed into an angel." We had a long discussion about whether the fight was genuine. Had Jacob really struggled? Wasn't it the transposition of a mystical trial related after the event as an actual happening?

"If Jacob invented this fight, why is he wounded? Was it self-mutilation?" I asked.

"No," he replied very definitely, "the wound is the proof that there was a fight."

The Nights of Lutetia is a novel about the impossibility of naming. Shahar spoke to me at great length about Ludwig Wittgenstein, whom he quotes at the beginning of the novel. Like Delacroix, the Austrian philosopher was obsessed with his own identity. "Am I really the person who bears my name?" Wittgenstein was still asking himself this nagging question a few days before he died.

We promised to meet again. David Shahar died on 2 April 1997. He took the secret of the name to his grave.

The question of Henry Delacroix left me with the same feeling of frustration. When observing a family, one should always concentrate on the most reserved member of the group. In the case of the Delacroix family, it is undoubtedly Henry. His self-effacement is easy to explain: this brother of the painter died at the Battle of

Friedland, as mentioned earlier. In about three days he would have been twenty years old. Thanks to the mayor of Contault, I learned that he belonged to the Seventh Regiment of Mounted Chasseurs, Fifth Company.

I went to the Military Archives at Vincennes to find out more. I was handed a large ledger bound in cracked shagreen leather. I found that he joined his regiment on 1 October 1806. He became a corporal on 1 January 1807, quartermaster sergeant on 1 February, then sergeant-major on 1 April of the same year. He will not rise above the rank of noncommissioned officer. Henry belonged to the light cavalry. He would have charged the enemy brandishing a saber with a thirty-five-inch-long curved blade. He should also have had a carbine attached to his shoulder belt and a pistol in his saddle holster.

The Friedland site today is a delightful place. The River Alle gently winds its way through a rolling green landscape. The whole battle was played out in a bend in the river around the village of Friedland. Henry Delacroix died during Grouchy's charge, which smashed the Russian army. I find this absence of *connaissances*, any tracks left by him quite disconcerting. But then, what trace could remain of a young person who died nearly two centuries ago in Eastern Prussia? The physical description provided by the military documents is obviously minimal. Henry had blue eyes. He was rather tall for those days: five feet, nine inches.

Why take an interest in Henry rather than in Charles-Henry, the eldest? A researcher, Dr. Jean-Luc Stéphant, has followed Charles-Henry's career and garnered quite a few disturbing elements.[2] The question of the brother for someone like Delacroix, who identifies with Jacob, is definitely worth considering. Jacob the wrestler at Jabbok fooled Esau for the first time when he tricked his elder brother into selling his birthright for a pottage of lentils, and for the second time when he wrongfully received his father's blessing.

Eugène Delacroix was only nine years old when Henry died at Friedland. There is nothing to indicate any rivalry between these two brothers. As far as Charles-Henry is concerned, some kind of conflict seems more plausible. (A persistent but false claim suggests that he is the model for Philippe Bridau, a character in Balzac's *La Rabouilleuse*.) Jean-Luc Stéphant has shown, however, that Charles-Henry Delacroix, aide-de-camp to Prince Eugène and seriously wounded in the retreat from Russia, could not really be taken for the degenerate Philippe Bridau. Nevertheless, like Balzac's hero, the painter's elder brother did come down in the world by marrying a girl who worked at an inn. It is also interesting to note that Charles-Henry was married at Louroux in Touraine, in the church of Saint-Sulpice.

Yet a close reading of *La Rabouilleuse* reveals certain characters that have some significance for anyone interested in the Delacroix family. Joseph Bridau is a painter of genius, generous, hot-blooded, very poor, and absorbed in his art, which is finally recognized and acclaimed. In spite of that fame he is still affected by his unhappy childhood, as his mother did not hide her preference for his brother Philippe. She had married a high-ranking civil servant of Napoleon's Empire, but was widowed very early with two young children.

Balzac points out that she also had a difficult childhood, hated by a father who believed she was a child conceived in adultery. It is clear that the author of *La Comédie humaine*, who dedicated *La Fille aux yeux d'or* to Eugène, knew the story of the Delacroix family and used some facts to create the portrait of Agathe Bridau and her two sons. Balzac even gives the game away in *Entre Savants*, a sketch attached to *La Comédie humaine* concerning Joseph Bridau. He mistakenly calls him Eugène Bridau.

On 15 July 1850, Delacroix writes out a whole passage from *La Rabouilleuse* in his *Journal*. He must have liked that extract, although it has nothing to do with the family situation of the Bridaus. As with Talleyrand and Charles Delacroix, he quotes and nothing more. Impassive as usual. When *La Rabouilleuse* was published in 1841, everyone had made the connection—except Delacroix. *He does not want to know*. This refusal can be interpreted as provocative or ironical. He knows that everyone else knows. But he does not care. And he refuses to remain silent. He will not avoid mentioning particular names or facts. With the sangfroid that is so characteristic of him, Delacroix dissembles and plays on what is implied or insinuated. It is his way of keeping people at arm's length, of defying everything while being aware that the taboo still exists. It is a way of freeing himself for a moment while still being a prisoner of the secret.

In actual fact, everything began at Augerville, the château where Delacroix stayed several times while he was working on the Chapel of the Holy Angels. It was at Augerville that the story of his birth was first put about by Mme. Jaubert, who regularly attended the musical evenings that included the painter. Her *Souvenirs*, in which she insinuates that Talleyrand was Eugène's father, show that she observed him closely during these gatherings. All her absurd carrying-on so that she can follow Delacroix like a bloodhound, yapping with delight as she catches sight of a bone, is not even funny.

The park, which Delacroix sketched several times, still looks handsome. The property has been bought by a Japanese company and turned into an eighteen-hole golf course. The inside of the château is another story entirely. The rooms are now desolate and decayed.

I had the honor of inspecting the château and the golf course with Mr. Kameyama, who suffered in silence as he showed me the unfinished buildings. "We had to stop work on the club house. The crisis in Japan began very early and finished late," he said, lamenting the state of things.

There are still many traces of troubadour style in the château. Medieval coats of arms grace walls and fireplaces. The wind whistles through many of the dilapidated rooms; some of the holes have been blocked up with plastic bags. "When the crisis is over, we'll do the repairs," Mr. Kameyama kept repeating, unable to hide his embarrassment. In the meantime, the restaurant and bar had been set up in the Renaissance outbuildings. It is impossible to identify Delacroix's room on the first floor. What happened to the frescoes he thought were seventeenth century?

After Berryer died in 1868, Augerville had a succession of owners. They had hardly bought it before they wanted to get rid of it. I found out that the founder of my French publishing house, La Table Ronde, spent the whole of his childhood in the Château d'Augerville.

Last I heard, the Japanese had sold the property. A French company has acquired it. The crisis is over. It seems that Augerville will come into its own again.

CHAPTER 17

Jacob's Eye

I have an appointment with the sacristan to see the two wooden angels. They were discovered a few years ago in the church crypt, where relics of the earlier church built in the twelfth century are enshrined.

I have the unpleasant feeling that Delacroix sometimes lets down his guard only to set me on the wrong track. Could he have become my adversary, my opponent? "There was something of the rebellious angel who redeems his soul through the greatness of his genius," wrote Arsène Houssaye, the novelist, essayist, and contemporary of the painter.[1] The rebellious angel. With Delacroix it is impossible to get away from these heavenly creatures. The poem by Baudelaire, which the lecturer is so fond of quoting, emphasizes this maleficent aspect of the man: "Delacroix, evil angels haunt this lake of blood."

We have hardly entered the crypt when the light goes out. After my initial reaction to this rather unpleasant surprise, I try to get my bearings. In the darkness I can sense the slow-breathing church above me exhaling a smell of marshlands. Children's voices mingle with this background noise, which can be mistaken for silence. It is actually a dull soft rumble, a barely perceptible murmur.

The reappearance of the light was enough to change the smell of the crypt. It now seems like overripe fruit. The underground

world laid out before me is made up of passageways, little grot-
toes, and huge rooms lit by light from small basement windows.
With their ventilation shafts and their steps, these catacombs
resemble an abandoned quarry. The large, rough bases of the pillars, which look as if they have been hewn with pickaxes, make
me feel vaguely uneasy. They could be elephant's feet, a forest of
hooves about to move. I could be trampled underfoot.

The sacristan leads the way. The maze is in the reverse image
of the church above us, but it is distorted, the perspective of the
walls and ceilings is truncated and out of shape.

We are now at the heart of Saint-Sulpice, in the nocturnal,
primitive part where its life begins. It is deep in the shadows of
this cave that Saint-Sulpice grew, and prospered, close to the element of water in a well that was built like a tomb.

Before the Revolution, the crypt was used as a cemetery. It is
estimated that about five thousand people are buried in the foundations. I'm told that the underground area had the advantage of
drying out the bodies and preserving them. In the choir you can
still see the trapdoor where the bodies were lowered down into
the crypt. Mme. de Lafayette, Molière's wife Armande Béjart,
Racine's tragedienne La Champmeslé, and Montesquieu were
all buried in this underground vault. During the Terror, the
graves were desecrated by the revolutionaries who used the lead
from the coffins to make bullets. In a corner above a small opening, there is a sign indicating an ossuary. I can see a dusty heap of
lime and humus. It gives off a smell like a damp floorcloth.

Some of the rooms are enclosed with iron railings. Broken pillars, capitals lying on the ground, funerary columns, sarcophagi:
this world beyond the grave is just like the *latomes*, the quarries
used as prisons in Greece. In the middle of this incredible jumble,
I come across an inscription written on a piece of cardboard:

"Here lies Louise-Élisabeth d'Orléans, Queen of Spain, died 16th June 1742." Who wrote this epitaph? It looks recent. This church has been rebuilt and founded again and again, and its foundations are indelibly marked by what has been lost and left unfinished— the head priest Languet de Gergy could finish the work only with the help of a lottery. The fragments of architecture, the tomb-stones, the darkness and the ruined splendor of the mausoleum vie with one another in arousing thoughts of privation and imprisonment. Standing in this necropolis, I suddenly remember the broken statuary and plaster I have seen in the attic space over the loggia and the architectural ruins imagined by Servandoni.

This world still oppresses me. It still haunts me, even in my dreams. But why should these obsessions suddenly surface now, here, in the underground foundations of the church? Voices, sighs, whispers, locked rooms, unseen animals...A man who has been tortured screaming in the night, a rattle of chains, a moan, the banging of iron doors, the footsteps of our guards. The soundscape fades out; the empty space fills with the white silence of the prison.

The sacristan, preoccupied with other things, turns and looks at me. My face is pale. "Pay no attention to the mess!" he says, and his simple, friendly words help me regain my composure and begin to breathe easily again.

We are in the crypt theater, also called the Saint-Just Room. Performances are regularly put on there. It is said that, during the Revolution, Saint-Just held meetings there when he was deputy for the Aisne at the Convention. Saint-Just, "the archangel of the Revolution." The heavenly militia has certainly taken over Saint-Sulpice, which was also a revolutionary church, although that fact is often forgotten.

The small room the sacristan has just opened is a shambles. A stale smell of dust with hints of earth and damp waft out to greet us. Wobbly chairs, broken chandeliers, nativity-scene figures lie stranded on the ground. In the middle of this hospice where all the surviving old wares of Saint-Sulpice have landed up, two supernatural creatures suddenly appear.

It really is like an apparition. Two perfect beings. They have made themselves visible for me and my friend the sacristan, but then again, this is not unusual for angels. Perfect beings? I should be more precise. The skin coloring of the two statues is quite dark. In addition to that, they are damaged, like all the objects in this junk room. The left wing is missing on both angels. The handsomer of the two—the other is rather chubby cheeked— has lost his right forearm. But what a gentle, serene expression he has. In spite of their infirmities, the angels spread their calming presence over all the disorder around them.

Their original home was the former church of Saint-Denis-de-la-Chartre on the Île de la Cité, framing the high altar. They disappeared during the Revolution, and were eventually tracked down in a second-hand dealer's shop by the priest at Saint-Sulpice, who placed them in the middle of the choir. They later stood at the entrance to the Chapel of the Holy Virgin then, in 1860, on each side of the altar of the Assumption.

Delacroix saw the two dark archangels. There is no mention of them in his writings, but it stands to reason that having spent such a long time at Saint-Sulpice, he must have become familiar with every detail in the church.

The sacristan is looking at me with a puzzled expression on his face: I keep walking around the angels, looking at their heads, standing back then moving closer again. An absurd thought has just come into my mind.

"Look. Don't you see a resemblance?"

"A resemblance? To whom?"

He thinks again and looks at me. He understands what I mean and begins to smile. He is probably thinking that one shouldn't argue with obsessives, that it's better to humor them.

"You're obviously thinking of Delacroix's angel."

"You must admit that there is a family resemblance. The more I look at them, the more unsettling I find the relationship between the two."

"Perhaps. But angels are always represented in the same way: the position of the wings, the rather feminine hairstyle."

"I'm talking of the face: the nose, the chin, the way the eyes are set. Quite apart from the hair and the shape of the wings."

"Yes, perhaps..."

He looks at me with an indulgent smile. He must be touched by my enthusiasm.

They really are dark for angels. I wonder if it were not for this reason that they were buried in the depths of Saint-Sulpice.

"Buried! You're going a bit too far there. They had to be stored somewhere. And I don't know when they were put in that cellar."

Exactly! Why put them in the deepest, darkest heart of the church? Was the beauty of the two angels relegated to the underground area too disturbing? Saint-Denis-de-la-Chartre, where the statues originally stood, used to be a prison. The church was knocked down. Then the wandering life of the two heavenly creatures began. Heavenly? Should such radiant beings be shut up in Hades?

As it says in the Second Epistle to the Corinthians, "Satan himself is transformed into an angel of light." Lucifer was the most beautiful and the first among the angels. Pride made him fall and cast him forever into the eternal flames. The threatening shadow of the two angels hangs over Delacroix's wall.

*   *   *

I want to be sure in my mind about all this. I go up to the ground floor again and hurry over to the Chapel of the Holy Angels. Bursting in as though about to conduct a search, I come face to face with…Léopold and the lecturer from the Louvre. What a coincidence! They seem to know each other well. Curiously enough, they don't look surprised to see me. Léopold says solemnly, "We were waiting for you."

"How did you know I'd be coming?" I reply with a hint of uneasiness in my voice.

"Oh! That's easy. You were looking at the crypt. I knew that you'd stop here when you came up again," Léopold said, gazing at his hands the way particularly tough policemen do in films.

"Who told you I was down in the crypt?"

"Everything gets around in Saint-Sulpice. It's a little village! Did you see those two angels?"

"I was just coming to check on a detail," I reply, looking at him suspiciously.

I hesitate to tell them about my tour of the crypt. I'm still stunned by this chance meeting, and the complicity of the man and the woman intrigues me.

A light like a broad stretch of rippling water flows through the window and shimmers in the chapel. The angel is bathed in the great flood of light. His hair shines in the sunshine. The nose, the shape of the face, and the hair certainly remind one of the angels in the crypt.

One thing suddenly becomes clear from the presence of Léopold and the lecturer: I'm too close to it. I've stayed with my nose pressed to the wall for too long. I must keep my distance if I want to solve this puzzle. Once you go into the chapel, you are trapped, locked in by the two side panels. Once you start examining *Wrestling with the Angel* and *Heliodorus*, you are caught.

This chapel has an extraordinary power to draw you in. The caravan just about to disappear into the pass in the background of
the painting is the prime example of the way it pulls you into
the picture. I had already experienced how *Wrestling with the
Angel* can engulf the viewer when I was on the mobile scaffolding. The rising tide of light made me think of it.

Léopold has put on his smart sunglasses. The lecturer is looking impatient, blinking her eyes in the glare of the liquid fire
now blazing in the window. Such a broad, blinding flow of light
seems to make the chapel rise. You would think that Delacroix
had opened the great floodgates of the ocean, covering everything.

We stand there in silence; the sight has left us speechless. It is
only when the light seems to be waning that Léopold breaks the
silence.

"The banks have burst.... It's overflowing! Strange things
always happen in this chapel."

"What's overflowing? I don't follow you!"

"It's obvious! You're on the wrong track," he whispers. "I
warned you earlier."

The wrong track? How much could he know about the objec-
tives I've been pursuing? And why does he use that tone with
me? He says that I must free myself from the hold that Delacroix
has on me. He leads me over to the giant shell that Pigalle put on
top of his white marble base. He speaks softly.

"Look at this shell. It comes from Oceania. The Venetian
Republic presented it to François I. It's a man-eating species of
giant clam. Delacroix often looked at it. He even used Pigalle's
pedestal to draw the base of one of the three trees—the one in
the foreground. Man eating. Do you understand?"

He speaks excitedly about the obscure origins of *Jacob Wrestling with the Angel.* I finally realize, from what he is saying, that Delacroix was inspired by a painting by Titian, *The Martyrdom of Saint Peter.*

"That painting has an incredible history. Think of it! Stolen by Napoleon, given back after Waterloo, reinstalled in the Church of San Giovanni and San Paolo in Venice, then it disappeared during a fire in 1869. It was thought to have been destroyed. Who took it? No one knew. Not a sign of it for a century, until it reappeared on the illegal market. They say it's now in Zurich. The starting point, the very essence of *Wrestling with the Angel* is in this painting that did not really disappear. The trees, the titanic struggle, everything is there."

He explains to me with a mysterious look on his face that the master painter of the Holy Angels is no Tom Thumb, and that he is not the type to leave a trail of white pebbles to lead me back home. On the contrary, he has put on seven-league boots to keep nuisances well away from Jabbok.

"You've obviously realized that this chapel is not very angelic at all."

What do these insinuations and thinly veiled warnings mean? The lecturer is standing apart from us under the organ loft. She is not taking part in our conversation, but she looks uneasy and her rather nervous expression shows that she knows what we are talking about.

Léopold is trying to give me some explanations. Why is he stressing the original designation of the Holy Angels? Delacroix thought that it was called the Font Chapel. He had therefore chosen subjects not only to do with baptism but also with original sin and atonement.

"Do *you* believe in original sin?" he asks with some hesitation.

"There's no question about believing in it or not," I reply. "It's like the air: it obviously exists, although it's true that one can't see it."

"It obviously exists! You know that it's a concept invented by Saint Augustine."

"Call it what you will: the fall, the loss of innocence. It has been the sign of our imperfection since Creation. We are forever at war with ourselves. The problem of evil! You know what Pascal said: 'Without this mystery, the most difficult to understand of all, we cannot possibly understand ourselves.'"

"In any event, Delacroix believed in original sin. As did Baudelaire. He must have felt frustrated at not being able to deal with the subject at Saint-Sulpice. Although..."

The lecturer is signaling to him. He replies by discreetly nodding his head in my direction.

"Original sin, evil, inherited corruption, whatever you like to call it. It permeates the walls of the Holy Angels. Lucifer's pride was certainly the cause of his fall. You should also think about Delacroix's pride. Who am I? How am I seen and judged? Everlasting human vanity! His certainty that he can control everything. It's terrible! There's no redemption—apart from his genius, the kindhearted will say. Well, I must go."

Léopold and the lecturer depart. Their footsteps echo in the church. I'm alone. I like listening to these soft solemn thuds on the stone floor worn smooth by so many feet. They resound in the vast interior of the church. All these familiar noises—the muffled clamor from outside, the padded door banging—lend color to the soundscape of Saint-Sulpice. They are as familiar to me as the architecture.

I feel quite at a loss. This chance meeting, their collusion, Léopold's uneasiness, the lecturer's annoyance. Strangely enough, she seemed less vehement than usual. For once she wasn't being pretentious. Her nervous tension had not disappeared, but I was no longer the object of it. What were they trying to tell me?

The candles in the Chapel of the Souls in Purgatory are going out. A smell of mutton fat released by the black tips of their smoking wicks drifts in my direction. The lecturer once mentioned "the underworld" when speaking about the chapel Heim painted. The brightness of the Holy Angels suddenly seems almost indecent. When the church was divided up, Heim was given something like Hades, the lower world, the nether region. But in the end, he may be the one who has the real prize.

I don't feel like following Léopold's advice. I come back to the Chapel of the Holy Angels. Leaning against the wall, I look once again at the two paintings. It's the best vantage point and also a way of keeping my distance to avoid being drawn in. *Wrestling with the Angel* seems so calm, so glowing and transparent. I become aware of the silent movement in the three great trees and the deep breath of wind blowing the Temple curtains. They are like a background of quiet meditation.

My attention is drawn to Jacob's eye. I had never seen it so bulging before. This wild stare could be explained by the effort he is expending, and yet the black spot of the pupil expresses not only energy but also strong emotion. And this emotion looks very much like fear. Who then is this opponent who makes Jacob's eye protrude so much? Is this one Cyclopean eye a warning? All the supernatural power of the painting comes from this nasty, disturbing gaze. The diabolical element of *Wrestling with the Angel* is surely concentrated in that black look?

This small point of frenzy surrounded by the light falling on Jabbok changes everything. Could it be that Delacroix had subverted the scene from the Scriptures, well before Gauguin, whose *Vision after the Sermon* distorts the episode from Genesis? It would not be the first time.

Jacob is shown not as the character from the Bible, but as a mythological hero. Like Hercules, he wears a lion skin across his shoulder. One of the paws can be seen flying in the air near his right calf. The angel is an impassive sun god with a head like Apollo. He calls us to witness in the boldest way: by giving us the eye. He scarcely looks at his opponent and is only concerned with one thing: his accomplice, the viewer.

He had already altered the original meaning in his first great religious work, *Christ in the Garden of Gethsemane*. This painting from 1824 is in the church of Saint-Paul & Saint-Louis in Paris. Knowing he is about to be arrested, Christ prays, "Father, if thou be willing, remove this cup from me." An angel then appears from heaven to comfort Christ. Delacroix changed this event in a very strange way. Instead of welcoming the angels, Christ rejects them, and to emphasize his point, Delacroix portrayed not one but three angels. The son does not want anything to do with his father's messengers. The gesture he makes with his hand is unmistakable, almost indecent: Christ is quite simply sending them packing, "They can go to the Devil!" is what he seems to be saying. One can see that the poor angels begin to weep not because they are thinking of the victim's torture and suffering to come, but because they are being turned away in the worst possible manner.

In his *Vision after the Sermon*, Gauguin takes up the theme of *Jacob Wrestling with the Angel* but makes the angel look demonic. The poet Lautréamont settled in Paris in 1867. Was he thinking of Delacroix's painting when he wrote the second song of *Maldoror?* Maldoror insists on kissing the mouth of the exhausted angel. In the end he strangles him. "He leans over and lays his wet, salivary tongue on the cheek of the angel, who stares at him with pleading eyes."

In the Delacroix Museum in rue Furstenberg there are several of the painter's notebooks from the time when he was working at the Holy Angels. He used them to list what he spent on art materials, coal, and cigars. There is an angel's wing at the bottom of the last page in one of these notebooks with their speckled blue covers. It is not a proper sketch. Delacroix seems to have drawn it absentmindedly, as one doodles in the corner of a page.

This wing is black. Its outline is hooked and excessively jagged. It is not an angel's wing.

CHAPTER 18

The Sybil and the Golden Bough

A portrait by Nadar says a lot about the blackout of information that the old artist wanted to impose at the end of his life. Nadar, photographer of the famous, was a neighbor of Delacroix's at Champrosay. He lived in L'Hermitage, a fine house in the middle of a forest, which Delacroix admired enormously. ("What I need is a manor house just like that," he declares with a hint of envy.)

Nadar took the painter's photograph in his last years. It is a striking snapshot. The closed, impenetrable expression more than ever prevents any sign of spontaneity. It is unique. In spite of the pose, which also does not permit the slightest relaxation, one can still make out some features in all that rigidity. Delacroix once copied an appalling sentence into his *Journal*: "I will die ashamed of having been a man." The photograph has caught an impassive face with no expression apart from one barely perceptible crease. Does it express defiance or disgust? There is something inhuman in this indifferent posture, which could also be a form of bravado. A proud, disenchanted old man scornfully eyes the world he is about to leave, even though he has few illusions about the other life. ("What shall we find on the other side? Night, dreadful night.")

Another photograph by Petit from 1860 is more terrible still. The black leopard's gaze is colder than ever. The intensity of the narrowed eyes could almost be tender, but the stare is so piercing and gleams with such cruelty that one can hardly bear to look at it. Delacroix was too clear-headed not to be aware of the impression these photos make. He had asked Nadar to destroy these "miserable effigies."

On the invitations he sends out in July 1861, Delacroix states that the Chapel of the Holy Angels may be inspected "from Wednesday 31 July until Saturday 3 August only, from 1:00–5:00 o'clock in the afternoon." He gives a brief account of the original context of *Jacob Wrestling with the Angel* and *Heliodorus* by simply paraphrasing the Bible. Nothing about the ceiling that shows *The Archangel Michael Slaying the Demon*. A draft of the invitation card[1] shows that Delacroix originally intended to give a commentary on that painting: "The companions in revolt lie much farther away, beaten and dispersed. It [the demon] is still fuming with impotent rage, but a last stroke from the victorious archangel is about to hurl it into the abyss burning with God's anger." Why did he give up this explanation emphasizing God's anger? Commenting on the crossing of the Jabbok ford, he writes: "The holy books see this struggle as a symbol of the trials God sometimes sends His chosen ones." In what holy books did Delacroix find such an interpretation? There is nothing in the Old or New Testament to support his explanation, which is actually rather pedestrian.

Louis-Charles Timbal, who painted the Saint Geneviève Chapel in the ambulatory, describes Delacroix on the day of the unveiling as looking decidedly uneasy. He goes to meet his guests, a thin, sickly figure with his neck swathed as usual in an enormous scarf. Normally so self-assured, this time he cannot hide his agitation. "The master, his face pale and his lips trembling from some hidden anguish in his heart, was replying with a smile and words he did not seem to be aware he was uttering." We are not used to seeing Delacroix like this. But the chapel is his life's work, and he is waiting like a schoolboy for the authorities of the art world to give their assessment."

Théophile Gautier congratulates the artist. Admirers of the painter, like Théophile Thoré and Baudelaire, are loud in their praise, but there are some reservations in the conventional compliments given by certain other critics, such as Paul de Saint Victor or Louis Vitet. Saint Victor condemns the "iron-grey color" of the horse in *Heliodorus* and is openly disparaging about the ceiling. Delacroix is deeply wounded by his criticisms.

The chapel is of little interest to the officials, who have not bothered to come. Delacroix writes bitterly that "I have not had a visit from the minister, the prefect, Nieuwerkerke,[2] nor anyone from the court or from people in the appropriate high places, in spite of the invitations I have sent." A delegation from the École des Beaux-Arts sent to examine the decoration of the chapel declares on 27 August 1861: "The subcommittee found the work worthy of this artist's earlier output. It was interpreted with conscientiousness and talent."

Conscientiousness and talent! One may laugh at this sententious observation, but it is a reasonably accurate summary of contemporary opinion. When the parish priest of Saint-Sulpice asked Delacroix's permanent rival, Ingres, what he thought, the answer came: "Monsieur le curé, you can be sure of it—there is a hell." Very interesting, that reference to hell! What a pity that Ingres did not explain himself more fully.

Becoming increasingly gloomy, Delacroix takes refuge in his house at Champrosay. He spends most of his time there until his death on 13 August 1863.

Champrosay...I like walking in the old forest with the Seine on one side and the Yerres on the other. A certain Jeanne Poisson ran into it to cross the path of the king who was hunting there. That is how Louis XV met the future Marquise de Pompadour.

There is a great variety of remarkable trees in the Sénart woods: they include the 680-year-old Antin oak and the Prieur oak, felled in 1980, which Delacroix sketched in pencil on 13 May 1857. As we know, it was used as a study for the group of three great trees where the fight between Jacob and the angel takes place. Delacroix also did several sketches of the Antin oak, which he often mentions in his *Journal*.

Like him, I love going deep into this forest with its many pools, and seeing how delicately the light filters down through the foliage. Nature as depicted by Delacroix in *Wrestling with the Angel* is not very eastern—except for the part with the flocks. The stream, the vegetation, the rise with the three trees definitely belong to the landscape of the Île-de-France area around Paris. Whenever I see the painting of *Jacob Wrestling with the Angel*, I cannot help thinking of the Senart forest and the damp smell of its tall trees. The wall in the Chapel of the Holy Angels has an acidic odor of vegetation, like humus from the primitive world, which one can still breathe in the air of some secluded paths. Delacroix loved to wander in the woods and squelch around in the thick mud, observing the decomposing organic matter, "the living, universal melting pot." He always had a saprophiliac side to his nature: a fascination with destruction and putrefaction.

The Antin oak he liked so much is still there—feeling its age a little, but still robust. In spring its foliage is thinner than that of the other trees, but there is still something jaunty in the way its sparse tresses float in the wind. The patriarch is definitely holding his own and will see many others dead and buried before he is. A few years ago some neighboring species of tree were ravaged by processionary caterpillars. The proud Antin oak stood firm: the only one not to succumb to the disease.

A notice calls upon visitors to "Please respect it." The trunk, treated with Stockholm tar, is hollow. Whenever I come to see it, I climb inside the split oak. The slightly moldy, musty bark makes me think of old cognac barrels. It seems like the ancient smell of time itself. Enclosed in the belly of the tree, I feel as if I am entering the forbidden cave and hearing the past murmuring all around me. The cries of children playing ball and the rustling of the leaves have disappeared. Only a vague continuous sound makes its way in through the wooden walls around me, disturbed from time to time by the creaking of the old carcass. It is something like the constant pressure of water on the timber framework of a boat. In these moments I have the illusion of going deep inside the wall at Saint-Sulpice, deep within the flow of time, and of escaping the nightmare of *Wrestling with the Angel*.

Yes, this painting has now become an ordeal, a torment! I've tried everything. Who is to say that the truth does not lie here in the heart of this moribund old tree trunk? Proserpina insists that to pass safely through Hell the golden bough must be found and plucked from the tree. Could it be hidden in the Antin oak, the tree that restores life and never dies? With this precious asset for his journey, Æneas has to go back in time to see his father again and hear the family secret from his lips. "It is Virgil's golden bough, which can only be found and plucked by someone led on by fate," Delacroix writes. He was very struck by this story, and painted it in *The Sybil and the Golden Bough*, shown in the Salon of 1845. "Deep in the dark forest, the golden bough, conquest of great hearts and God's favorites." The connection with *Wrestling with the Angel* is obvious. Didn't a critic once state that the painting in Saint-Sulpice was "the great Virgil's *lacryma rerum*"?[3]

The Sybil points to the magic branch. She is not hidden; quite the opposite. Just look up and pluck it.

Delacroix's house, on Route Nationale 448, is a small building enclosed by a wall built of that millstone so typical of the greater Parisian region. The entrance porch is less commonplace with its flagstones studded with round stones. They look like shining black gems. Weathering has split some of them. The large garden almost creates the illusion of living in the country. Champrosay is the very picture of the ideal suburbanite existence.

The owner greets me with that far-away look I know so well. It's not coldness, but the sign of a cautious, concentrating mind. At our first meeting he had only just bought Delacroix's house. At that time, the interior with its tiny rooms had seemed very somber—like the new owner. He was wearing a Carnaby Street-style, striped, black jacket, which he wore pulled in at the waist as they did in the 1970s. He showed me Delacroix's studio. I was struck by its lack of space, but I had to admit that it had the compensation of a good light well and a very high ceiling. I had walked around the garden overgrown with weeds, stopping beside a huge box bush, almost a tree, and probably the only thing remaining from Delacroix's day. In his *Journal*, Edmond de Goncourt describes the building as "the house of an impoverished village notary."

"What inspired you to buy this house?"

"Certainly not Delacroix," he replied. "In fact it would be rather the opposite."

"The opposite?"

"Yes. I'm a painter."

I asked if I could see his paintings. He refused categorically.

"Anyway, I'm not interested in the object produced."

"So, you must be a painter without an object or a subject?"

He did not pick up on my rather heavy irony.

"I'm an unknown painter and want to stay that way."

"You've never shown your work?"

"No," he replied with what sounded like a blunt refusal.

But he was not unpleasant: a little vacant at most.

"Do you know what painters dream of these days?" he asked.

"I don't know. Their work, I suppose...."

"No. They dream of money. Of money, Monsieur."

That was six years ago. I have often thought of the man at Champrosay and his long silences inspired by some personal sadness. When I came back from walking in the forest, I decided to ring at his door without any prior warning. He opens it, showing no surprise, as if he were expecting me. I find him changed: less unhappy, in fact almost eloquent. The house has also changed. Interior walls have been knocked down and the rooms are bright. The look of a cramped suburban house has disappeared.

"So, it's not so difficult living with Delacroix's ghost?"

He looks at me with lackluster eyes.

"I didn't estimate the strength of that presence. I would perhaps have hesitated for longer.... Delacroix rather lingers like a parasite in these walls. But we manage to live together in harmony. I don't think much about him, actually."

He remains silent for a moment, showing no emotion as he looks at me.

"You see, I'm impervious to all forms of imagination or feeling based on the past."

At the same time, there is a kind of fire within him, a restrained enthusiasm that he keeps to himself. I ask him if he likes Delacroix.

"Like him? Hmm...How does one deal with a painter like that? He's there, and one has to come to terms with him," he says, his eyes sad and his expression weary, almost showing distaste.

"The unavoidable character of Delacroix seems to bore you?"

"He's one of those men who have gone beyond a certain point. And that point places them in another sphere. It's not about levels of excellence. I hate hierarchies."

He agrees to show me Delacroix's studio on the first floor, which he now uses. The light coming into the room through the well in the ceiling is very bright indeed, almost white. The only thing left from the time when Delacroix worked there is a rather ugly earthenware heating stove. He painted many canvases in this room, including *Christ Sleeping during the Storm, Hamlet and Polonius, Christ in the Tomb*. Alphonse Daudet, who had broken his leg, also lived in this studio during the Franco-Prussian War in 1870. Daudet stayed for some time in Champrosay. His story seems to amuse the owner.

"Daudet didn't feel very much at home in this house. Delacroix's ghost must have worried him."

His works are all over the studio, forming a spectacle of kites, still life, a blue whale made of pieces of plastic and exceptionally beautiful....

"As you can see, I'm searching for a different space, something that hasn't been utilized yet. I won't show any of my work until I realize that ambition. I don't want to tell stories."

He looks at me without speaking for a moment. His voice suddenly changes.

"And what about you? I have the impression that you do want to tell stories. That's of no interest, believe me."

He looks upset, and his face still shows a trace of the unsociability he has managed to subdue, but which occasionally shows through. There is nothing aggressive in that bitterness; it is always melancholy. He has decided to confront people and circumstances with nothing but calm. I have the impression that he expects nothing. I feel as if I am facing Delacroix in his final phase....

He suddenly and deliberately looks me straight in the eye.

"You're searching! You know what you're looking for, I hope? Instead of scouring the countryside, beating woods and bushes, you should explore inside yourself. Delacroix, his house, his oak tree, his secret—that's for the tourist bureau. This heritage mania is the bane of our age."

His tone has become more passionate but he manages to check this strong streak of disillusion. It is like a voice that has suddenly come from elsewhere, as if someone were speaking through him: it has Delacroix's coldness together with the kindness that struck Baudelaire so forcibly. He has gone back into his lair. He says: "You're wasting your time here. All this fetishism with the past leads nowhere. Stop combing everything in Delacroix's wake! Forget him!"

I hear it as, "Forget me."

Epilogue

Like Æneas, I have descended into hell but, unlike Virgil's hero, I have not managed to return to the surface again. I am still wandering in the labyrinth. I have my familiar routine here. I continue to search. Heim, Delacroix, the angel: all three of them have combined to bar my way.

When Jacob's path was blocked, he broke through. From that moment, everything was clear, Jacob *understood*. He had accepted the fight because he was certain he would win.

Delacroix let him escape by changing the text from Genesis. Never has an angel been depicted so ambiguously, nor with so much irony. Would you want to extract a secret from someone who hardly takes you seriously? After all, the actual fight between Jacob and the angel never really interested Delacroix. In his painting he directed his attention only to the moment when Jacob asks the angel's name. "Tell me, I pray thee, thy name," Jacob asks. And the stranger replies, "Wherefore is it that thou dost ask after my name?"

The name, the obscure power of fate. Should he sign it with a *cross?* Delacroix, no one's son? And what of Heliodorus, who thinks he can so easily steal the treasure from the Temple! Things that are hidden can certainly be brought to light, but the person who reveals them puts himself in grave danger.

The angels with their whips do not hold back with their blows. The treasure has been violated, spilled on the ground. Gold and jewels spew forth from the caskets. Nevertheless, the most important thing is safe: the treasure has been profaned, but it has never been taken from the Temple—which must have pleased Delacroix. He eagerly signed his name in the middle of the scene depicting a disclosure and a whipping. It is also a way of making a rod for his own back. He said too much in *Jacob Wrestling with the Angel*; he punishes himself in *Heliodorus*.

I have been mistaken about Delacroix. I have confused the painter and the man. It would be foolish to maintain that his life was not up to the standard of his work. Baudelaire summed it up perfectly: "He was passionately in love with passion, and coldly determined to find the means of expressing passion in the most visible way."

Delacroix put his painting into his life, not the other way round. He was as ardent and controlled as his creations. Is he a romantic figure? His life was sustained by a single aim: to paint. He frequented high society, traveled a great deal, read a great deal. And love? He had no hesitation in writing to a woman: "I am of an age when needs, even those of the heart, are surplus to requirements when they compete with the demands of work."

Those are the only demands that counted for him. Even his hedonism—the care he took in choosing his wines, cigars, and food—had no other object than to keep the body going and provide energy so that he could paint without worrying about anything else. In some ways he is like Flaubert. He found his salvation in art, realizing his ambition through sacrifice, suffering, and hard work. There is something of the Christ of painting about Delacroix. To make the fires of inspiration burn ever brighter, he allowed his life to be consumed.

He padlocked everything: that was the way the secretive painter of *The Women of Algiers* always behaved. After all, he even saw the sexual act as a kind of closure. He hid his deep wound, barred the door to the secret rooms of his soul. But it was no use transforming an obstacle into a screen of fire in the Chapel of the Holy Angels: his Jacob got the better of him. *Wrestling with the Angel* is a real denial as well as a masterly evasion. In the end it is a demurrer, a blunt refusal. The whole drama of Delacroix is contained in that expression.[1] It is an end, a no, and the case is inadmissible.

At the same time as he was working on the Holy Angels, he painted *Ugolino and his Sons*. Taken from Dante's *Inferno*, the story concerns the ordeal of a father shut up in a tower with his children and condemned to death by starvation. Ugolino, the sole survivor, ultimately eats his sons' flesh. This story of a cannibal father obsessed Charles Delacroix's son, who was already contemplating the subject in 1847. He finished the painting in 1860, a year before the Holy Angels. Should this work be seen as a response to the question posed by *Wrestling with the Angel?*

When one is imprisoned by a wall, the only way to get out is to knock it down. In the Holy Angels, Jacob finally burst through the partition. He reached the other side. Heim was waiting for him.

What is it that continually puts me at odds with Delacroix in order to steer me elsewhere? The creator of *Wrestling with the Angel* has certainly had his revenge. I used him. I thought I could fill a void; all I did was make it larger. I have felt myself irresistibly dragged toward the neighboring chapel. While seeking the light of the Holy Angels, I have suddenly stumbled into the realm of darkness, among the paintings by Heim.

Delacroix drew me to him in order to make me lose my way with Heim, the creator of *Prayer for the Dead*. That is the reality of it.

How did I branch off to Heim, the anti-Delacroix? I was deceived by their complicity. After all, the most striking portrait of Delacroix was done in pencil by Heim, who caught him perfectly as a member of the institute with his stiff, haughty look. Heim! That way he has of following on behind Delacroix, taking up the theme of *Heliodorus* again, for example. "One wonders in what reign Monsieur Heim had talent," the critic Paul Mantz wrote maliciously at the time of the 1847 Salon. Baudelaire considered him "an eminent, distinguished artist, a searcher who misses being a fine genius by only a millimeter or a milligram of anything."

What a terrible thing to always fall short! Basically, he did not have the gift of grace. This is the painter I have chosen.

But where was Jacob hiding?

In the labyrinth I always thought that he would let me find the light again.

"It's a splendid picture. Unfortunately it's very damaged. We can't exhibit it to the public. It's somewhere in the stacks. The museum has only a tiny part of its collections on show."

"Could I see the painting?"

"With pleasure. But you'll have to be patient. I haven't had time to look at my records. It's either in the museum cellars or in the annex. Or even in the old cloakrooms. We're short of space. What can you expect? We're broke!"

It's an autumn day in Bordeaux. I have finally got round to visiting the Musée des Beaux-Arts to see Heim's painting, *The Arrival of Jacob in Mesopotamia*, which I had promised myself I would track down. Delacroix's neighbor in Saint-Sulpice was obsessed with Jacob. He painted him in another picture where the patriarch's sons bring him Joseph's coat.

I tell myself that Charles Delacroix is buried here in Bordeaux, and that the painter spent his infancy in the Palais de Rohan, but it's no use really. I no longer expect to discover anything. All these signs and portents have probably carried me too far.

There are still things that I do almost out of habit, as an escape. Heim's *Arrival of Jacob in Mesopotamia*—why not?

In my ignorance, I thought that the painting hung in one of the rooms in the museum. Seeing my disappointment, one of the attendants phones the office. I explain the purpose of my visit. The head curator comes down, probably touched by the interest I show in this picture. I can see that he is a very busy man. Nevertheless, he has decided to make himself available. I'm not sure that he understands what I'm looking for.

"I see," he says politely, "but are you interested in Delacroix or Heim?"

He is an efficient man with a sharp intelligence. He immediately engages the help of two employees.

"You'll be surprised. It's a big work: more than eight by nine feet. If I remember correctly, there is a wide band across the top where the painting has practically disappeared. It's an incomplete canvas."

"You mean that Heim never finished it?"

"What! You don't know? It was badly damaged in the 1870 fire."

"Did this fire have something to do with the war?"

"Yes, although only indirectly. The collections had been stored in the basement. It was very cold, the heater became white hot and set the place alight. Many paintings were badly affected by water."

We take a quick look in the former cloakroom of the museum. The curator rapidly surveys the room.

"Nothing but small pictures here. We'll go down to the basement."

It is a huge tunnel, and there are treasures stacked in this underground cave. One cannot see them properly due to insufficient space and funding. I suspect that the curator finds this lack of proper facilities humiliating. The sight of all these paintings, carefully stored and covered, sometimes makes him sigh and shrug his shoulders. We lift up dozens of canvases: Virgins with Child, Assumptions, mythological scenes. The two brawny men have become interested in the search and are marvelous at sorting the paintings and estimating their size. The curator also puts himself out, with the result that there are spider webs caught on his blazer. He is worried and finally says that the Heim must be in the annex.

The light has been cut off in the annex, and all we have are flashlights. There are crates everywhere waiting to be sent to Japan. After a long search, one of the employees calls out:

"I think we've found it."

He gently exhumes a huge painting from the darkness and takes off the cloth cover. A blackened part appears on which the flashlight casts a wan light. Small spots of mildew are dotted here and there all over it. There is not a sound in the huge dark room.

The two men slowly put the picture down against the wall. The frame does not look too bad. The curator, who was fiddling about with the electricity meter box, gives a triumphant cry. Neon light slices through the darkness around us.

And there, suddenly, is *The Arrival of Jacob in Mesopotamia.*

I'm speechless. What I was looking for is right in front of me.

I was chasing after Jacob, and he is here to meet me, traveler's staff in hand. In the sooty part, all I can see are shadows. There are shepherds resting in the shade of tall trees, pointing to a girl leading a flock: no doubt Laban's daughter. I like Jacob's hat. Very smart! It makes him look quite dashing. The curator explains that it's called a *petasus*. I prefer it to the planter's hat in

Wrestling with the Angel. An ancient temple or perhaps the walls of a Renaissance château can just be discerned in the background.

The canvas is out of shape, stiffened by mildew. I cannot take my eyes off the burnt strip, where lost figures seem to be moving about.

I have my Jacob. I should have started here, with this picture. It was not a painter's secret that I was trying to discover, but the secret of another man who one day found himself in the kingdom of darkness.

Will I come out into the light again? This must be the starting point: this black on the canvas, this destruction on which life will start again.... The curator turns to me and says:

"That missing section worries you! It's not a problem. We can restore what has been destroyed."

30 November 2000
Villa Jamot, Genthieu, Le Pouldu, Hoëdic (Le Vieux-Phare)

End Notes

FRONT MATTER

1. This text accompanied the invitation, sent out by the painter in July 1861, to inspect the Chapel of the Holy Angels in the church of Saint-Sulpice in Paris.
2. Genesis XXXII, 22–32.

CHAPTER I

1. The novel *Là-Bas* has been translated both as *Down There* and *Là-Bas: A Journey into the Self*.
2. Hosea XII, 4-5.
3. Jacques-Vincent Simmonnet, 1771 (manuscript housed in the Library of the Society of the Priests of Saint-Sulpice).
4. The *"veduta ideata."*
5. *Réflexion sur quelques cases de l'état présent de la peinture en France [Reflection on some causes of the present state of painting in France],* quoted by Émile Malbois.

CHAPTER 2

1. Maurice Barrès, *Le Mystère en pleine lumière [The Mystery in Full Daylight]*.
2. "Les Phares" ["Guiding Lights"], translated by Cyril Scott.
3. Psalm 69, verse 14.

CHAPTER 3

1. Romans 5:21.

2. A biblical allusion to bad feelings that ferment passion and give rise to sin in man, as sourdough rises in the oven. [Tr.]

CHAPTER 4
1. *Le Français*, 18 May 1871.
2. Quoted by Bruno Foucart in *Patrimoine et passions identitaires* [*Heritage and Issues of Identity*], under the chairmanship of Jacques Le Goff, published by Fayard.
3. Op. cit.
4. In Gaston Lemesle, *L'Église de Saint-Sulpice*.

CHAPTER 5
1. Condemned to death in 1815, he was visited by his daughter and wife, who took his place. He then escaped from prison disguised as a woman.
2. The legitimists were upholders of the senior branch of the Bourbon family, deposed in 1830. [Tr.]
3. The Prince de Condé, called Le Grand Condé, was one of the greatest generals in the reign of Louis XIV. The Fronde was an unsuccessful uprising of the nobles against Mazarin during Louis XIV's minority. [Tr.]

CHAPTER 6
1. [*An Attempt at an Exhaustive Description of a Place in Paris*]
2. *L'Église de Saint-Sulpice*.

CHAPTER 7
1. "The Work of General (Dr.) Camelin" (*Bulletin of the Aix Historical Society*, July-October 1979).
2. *Ange* in French means angel and was used as a Christian name. [Tr.]

CHAPTER 8

1. *Delacroix, les plus belles pages.*

2. A clump of dilated veins in the spermatic chord.

3. *Delacroix et Baudelaire.*

4. Letter to Jules Troubat, 1866.

5. Report number 281 (3 February 1976).

CHAPTER 10

1. Jean-Paul Kauffmann was kidnapped and kept in solitary confinement for three years while working as a journalist in Lebanon. [Tr.]

2. A political assembly set up by the Constitution of Year III (1795), and one of the two chambers forming the legislative body.

3. Robert Couffignal, *La Lutte de Jacob avec l'Ange.*

CHAPTER 11

1. A. Camelin, "Faut-il remettre en cause la naissance de Eugène Delacroix" ["Should the qustion of Eugène Delacroix's birth be reexamined"], *Histoire des sciences médicales,* vol. XII, no. 2, 1978.

CHAPTER 12

1. *Emmaus.*

2. *Dimanche m'attend.*

3. Yvan Christ, *Le Faubourg Saint-Germain.*

4. *En route.*

5. *L'Homme en secret.*

CHAPTER 13

1. In Gaston Lemesle, *L'Église de Saint-Sulpice,* op. cit.

2. *Société d'histoire de l'art français* (1992).

CHAPTER 14

1. A secret dungeon accessible only by a trapdoor.

CHAPTER 15

1. *Le Désenchantement du monde* (Gallimard).

CHAPTER 16

1. Translated from the Hebrew by Madeleine Neige, 1992 (François Bourin-Julliard).

2. "Chili et le frère 'oublié' d'Eugène Delacroix," by Dr. Jean-Luc Stéphant, in the *Bulletin de la Soci*été de l'histoire de l'art français, 1990.

CHAPTER 17

1. Quoted by René Huyghe in *Le Combat solitaire*.

CHAPTER 18

1. The Claude-Roger Marx Archives.

2. Director of the Imperial Museums.

3. Louis-Édouard Fournier, *Revue des arts décoratifs*, July 1901.

EPILOGUE

1. The author uses a legal expression here (*une fin de non-recevoir*) and emphasizes its meaning in the context of Delacroix by taking the phrase apart: *fin* (end), *non* (no), *recevoir* (to receive). [Tr.]

Bibliography

WRITTEN WORKS BY DELACROIX

Journal (1822–1863) (Plon, 1980).

Correspondance générale. 5 vols (Plon, 1936-1938).

Dictionnaire des Beaux-Arts. Edited by Anne Larue (Hermann, 1996).

Écrits sur l'art (Librairie Séguier, 1988).

Lettres intimes (Gallimard, 1954).

Souvenirs d'un voyage dans le Maroc (Gallimard, 1999).

Nouvelles Lettres (William Blake & Co., 2000).

ON DELACROIX

Daguerre des Hureaux, Alain: *Delacroix* (Hazan, 1993).

Delacroix. No. 408 of the review *Europe*, April 1963.

Deslandres, Yvonne: *Delacroix* (Hachette, 1963).

Escholier, Raymond: *Delacroix peintre, graveur, écrivain.* 3 vols (H. Floury, 1926–1929).

———, *Delacroix et les femmes* (Fayard, 1963).

Eugène Delacroix. In the series Génies et Réalités (Hachette, 1963).

Florenne, Yves: *Delacroix, les plus belles pages* (Mercure de France, 1963).

Gillot, Hubert: *E. Delacroix* (Les Belles Lettres, 1928).

Guégan, Stéphane: *Delacroix et les Orientales* (Flammarion, 1994).

Huyghe, René: *Delacroix ou le Combat solitaire* (Hachette, 1964).

Jobert, Barthélemy: *Delacroix* (Gallimard, 1997).

Jullian, Philippe: *Delacroix* (Albin Michel, 1963).

Loppin, Paul: *Les Grandes figures champenoises: Charles et Eugène Delacroix* (Pierre Béarn, 1963).

——, *Eugène Delacroix, l'énigme déchiffrée* (Pierre Béarn, 1965).

——, *Delacroix, père et fils* (Pierre Béarn, 1973).

Moss, Armand: *Delacroix et Baudelaire* (Nizet, 1973).

Planet, Louis de: *Souvenirs des travaux des peintures avec M. Eugène Delacroix* (Armand Colin, 1929).

Rautmann, Peter: *Delacroix* (Citadelles et Mazenod, 1997).

Regamey, Raymond: *Eugène Delacroix, Époque de la chapelle des Saints-Anges (1847–1863)* (Renaissance du Livre, 1931).

Rudrauf, Lucien: "De la bête à l'ange," Budapest, *Acta Historiæ Artium, Academiæ Scienti,* 1963.

Sérullaz, Maurice: *Les Peintures murales d'Eugène Delacroix* (Éditions du Temps, 1963).

——, *Delacroix* (Fayard, 1989).

Spector, Jack: *The Murals of Eugene Delacroix at Saint-Sulpice* (The College Art Association of America, 1967).

CATALOGS

Delacroix en Touraine. Tours, Musée des Beaux-Arts de Tours, William Blake & Co., 1998.

Delacroix, la naissance d'un nouveau romantisme. Rouen, Réunion des Musées nationaux, 1998.

Delacroix, les dernières années. Rouen, Réunion des Musées nationaux, 1998.

Delacroix: peintures et dessins d'inspiration religieuse. Nice, Réunion des Musées nationaux, 1986.

ON THE CHURCH OF SAINT-SULPICE

Boinet, André: *Les Églises parisiennes*, vol. II (Minuit, 1962).

De pierre et de cœur. Catalogue of the exhibition on Saint-Sulpice organized by the municipality of the 6th *arrondissement*, 1996.

De pierre et de cœur, l'église Saint-Sulpice, 350 ans d'histoire (Le Cerf, 1996).

Dreyfuss, Bertrand: *Le Guide du promeneur, VIe arrondissement* (Parigramme, 1994).

Hamel, Charles: *Histoire de l'église Saint-Sulpice* (Libraire Victor Lecoffre, 1900).

Lemesle, Gaston: *L'Église Saint-Sulpice* (Bloud et Gay, 1931).

Malbois, Émile: *Saint-Sulpice* (manuscript in the archives of the Company of the Priests of Saint-Sulpice).

Saint-Sulpice. Booklet with preface by the parish priest of Saint-Sulpice, Paul Roumanet, 2000.

ON JACOB WRESTLING WITH THE ANGEL

Barrès, Maurice: *Le Mystère en pleine lumière* (Plon-Nourrit, 1926).

Blanchard, Pierre: "Jacob et l'Ange," *Études carmélitaines*, Desclée de Brouwer, 1957.

Couffignal, Robert: *La Lutte de Jacob avec l'Ange* (Université de Toulouse-Le Mirail, 1977).

Deforges, Régine: *Lola et quelques autres* (Fayard, 1993).

Emmanuel, Pierre: *Jacob* (Le Seuil, 1970).

France, Anatole: *La Révolte des Anges* (Calmann-Lévy, 1914).

Gide, André: *Les Faux-Monnayeurs*, part 3 (Gallimard, 1925).

Jacob, les aléas d'une bénédiction (Labor et Fides, 1992).

Molinié, M.-D.: *Le Combat de Jacob* (Le Cerf, 1967).

Sébastien, Robert: *La Chapelle des Saints-Anges* (Plon, 1928).

Thomas, Jean-François and Bez, Michel: *L'Ardent Combat* (François-Xavier de Guibert, 1996).

MISCELLANEOUS

Alexis, M.: *Givry-en-Argonne* (no name of publisher, 1977).

Foucart, Bruno: *Le Renouveau de la peinture religieuse en France (1800–1860)* (Arthéna, 1987).

Hurel, Abbé A.: *L'Art religieux contemporain* (Librairie académique Didier et Cie, 1868).

Le Goff, Jacques: *La Naissance du Purgatoire* (Gallimard, 1981).

Poisson, Georges: *Saint-Maurice, l'histoire de notre ville*. Edited by Culture et Loisirs de la Ville de Saint-Maurice, 1992.

BOOKLETS AND ARTICLES

"Architecture et décors peints," Amiens, *Actes des colloques de la direction du Patrimoine* (Ministry of Culture), 1989.

Buttet, Patrick de: *Autour du berceau d'Eugène Delacroix*. 2 vols (Ville de Saint-Maurice, 1998).

Guillotin, Sonia: *L'Église de Corps-Nuds*. Monograph, (UF Environnement).

"Les Écrivains de Saint-Sulpice," *Le Promeneur des Lettres*.

Lveders, K. et al: "Le Grand Orgue de Saint-Sulpice et ses organistes," *La Flûte harmonique*, special no. 59–60, 1991.

Portal, Michel: *L'Urbanisme parisien au siècle des Lumières: la place Saint-Sulpice* (Action artistique de la Ville de Paris).

Wittmer, Pierre: *Sur les pas de Delacroix à Champrosay* (Agence culturelle et technique de l'Essonne).

The lines about the north tower in Chapter I (The Servandoni Towers) are by Georges Rose. Last works: *Rivages* (Le Dé Bleu, 1997); *L'Usage du ciel* (Souffles, 1997); *Moments* (Valenciennes, Cahiers Froissart, 1998).